Paradise, Newfoundland...

When I Walked Its Gravel Road

CHES
PENNELL

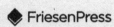

FriesenPress

One Printers Way
Altona, MB, R0G0B0
Canada

www.friesenpress.com

ISBN
978-1-03-911531-6 (Hardcover)
978-1-03-911530-9 (Paperback)
978-1-03-911532-3 (eBook)

1. BIOGRAPHY & AUTOBIOGRAPHY, PERSONAL MEMOIRS

Distributed to the trade by The Ingram Book Company

Table of Contents

Acknowledgements

To the old folks who lived in the Paradise of my youth, I thank you. Without you, I would not have my wonderful story to tell.

To my wife, Jan, who was with me every step of the way as I compiled my recollections.

To the youth of the current Paradise, I dedicate this book to you so you may know, and benefit from reading about, the humble beginnings of your thriving town.

Introduction

Paradise: the name itself stimulates the imagination. My Paradise, which I was born into midway through the twentieth century, wasn't a sun-drenched honeymoon destination, as the name may imply. What it was, however, was a tiny village onto itself, striving to thrive while experiencing all the growing pains that come with time. I was there during those growing pains, and I left after over twenty years, holding on to a box chock-full of varied memories.

My name is Ches, and I was part of that growth in the 1940s and 1950s, being born in a tiny house with a massive family proudly bearing the surname of Pennell. It was indeed a unique little part of the world living in its own bubble. Sitting practically on the doorstep of a then-major city called St. John's, our uniqueness was preserved, and our isolation was by choice. The colourful families were, to say the least, diversified. But we liked who we were, even if some others didn't. As Newfoundlanders, we have a unique and curious culture, and we are quite different from most other Canadian provinces. We hailed from hard-working stock of English and Irish settlers, who had raised our ancestors only an hour or so away from Paradise.

There were nineteen members of my family by the time it was all said and done in the mid-1960s, and every one of my siblings called our little old-fashioned bungalow home. Picture, if you will, a very long and dusty gravel road, fully wooded on both sides, except for the peppering of modest and sometimes irregular dwellings, each with a chimney laboriously puffing out its smoke from the wood-stoves. There were no poles for electricity, no sidewalks, and certainly no lawns, but scores of animals, people of every description, and all their various offspring. The families were normally big, and some personalities were even bigger.

The distinctive ways of Newfoundland living, with its own, sometimes odd, traditions, has practically vanished. Even though we all realize time must bring change, it's also a shame that the young people may never know how it was in Paradise's fledgling years.

It's my intention that this book will preserve the history of a place where so many lives are currently being lived with no inkling of Paradise's early days and how those early inhabitants coped. We must all remember the past to appreciate what was and to adjust to improve our future.

Adolescents today, including some of my own grandchildren, could hardly fathom a one-room schoolhouse with a woodstove smack-dab in the middle, churning out its only source of heat, which students had to keep lit from 8:00 a.m. to 3:00 p.m. I'm also sure that they couldn't grasp the concept of four siblings to a bed, having to chop and gather splits daily for the home woodstove in the kitchen for heat and cooking, doing without indoor plumbing (which meant hauling heavy buckets of water from your well and bathing once a week in a galvanized tub in the middle of your kitchen), gathering eggs from the henhouse, and going without snow-clearing, thermostats, telephones, and televisions. But in fairness, why would they? They didn't have to, but they can learn from that past and appreciate the future, with all its conveniences that is now theirs.

On the other hand, this generation won't know the sweetness of excitedly watching and waiting for chicks to gradually hatch in the barn, seeing a litter of kittens being born in your friend's porch, using a handmade slingshot that shoots perfectly straight, and the unmistakable aroma of homemade bread every day of the week. How well I remember the smells and sounds of newly sawed lumber at the mills, riding my grandfather's old horse after I helped the old gentleman pick weeds from his drills of crops and listened to his stories. Afterward, I often went skinny-dipping in the pond nearby to cool off with my buddies or brothers.

On the not-so-wholesome side, we grew up with some unsavoury characters. As a boy, I was always under the impression that Paradise housed its very own witch, who actually made her own birch brooms and who, for all intents and purposes, certainly fit the bill. We had thieves, madmen, horribly lazy individuals who didn't work a day in their lives, and homemade stills aplenty brewing their moonshine somewhere out of sight from Government officials.

Yet the majority of Paradise's people were anxious to get ahead, and with its nose to the grindstone, the community continuously pulled together, survived, and ultimately thrived.

In 1921, there were one hundred and fifty inhabitants putting down roots in Paradise, and by the 1950s, that number had increased by another hundred souls, myself included. Today, Paradise is an ultra-modern and bustling town that boasts a population of nearly 23,000.

So, as you read, you'll enter a portal to a time when Paradise was recognized as a tiny, struggling village. Learn about the people who called it home, where they came from, and what they called a normal day. You'll discover how exceptionally different, but also how remarkably *alike* every generation actually is in the long run. It's a historical, yet comical journey. I'm delighted to have been a vital part of it and look forward to taking you with me as we explore the Paradise of yesterday.

GRANVILLE

BILL & BEN MURPHY

Royal's Pond

P

GRANDFATHER PARSONS

HUSSEY'S

A

JOEY ROUNDBOY & JUL

ANDREW CLARKE

R

MARION LYNCH: CHARMER

A

MR. SHARPE'S BARN

D

FRIEND: TOMMY SHARPE

I

HOLY INNOCENTS'

S

BOG

PENNELL'S: MY HOUSE

E

GRANDFATHER RIXON

Rd.

ROY PARSONS

MABEL

UNCLE JIM RIXON

|FLINT|

| HILL |

_____TOPSAIL ROAD_____

The Island Of Newfoundland
Showing Location Of Paradise

The Island Of
New foundland
Showing Location
Of Paradise

Paradise, Newfoundland...
When I Walked Its Gravel Road

It's the mid-1950s, and I am one of seventeen children who will come into this world and grow up in the Pennell household in the tiny and unique town of Paradise. That little bungalow was built with love and precision by my father, Walter Pennell. Our town wasn't the modern and expansive Paradise of today. No Sir! Rather, it was a world away from the lined, neatly paved roads and sidewalks encircling the modern Paradise's sprawling subdivisions and thriving commercial enterprises.

Our family homestead was situated in basically the same location as the Paradise of today. However, it was only a fraction in size compared the huge and modern town it has become.

Travelling from St. John's, you entered our quaint little world from Topsail Road, where you would climb the extremely steep hill now known as Paradise Road. Back then, that steep incline was known as Flint Hill, and climbing it certainly wasn't for the faint of heart. With attention from the City Council crews over the years, the steepness has been gradually lessened. In the early days, the only road maintenance was done by a local and well-known resident by the name of Arch Sharpe. Armed only with a shovel and his horse, which he tackled to a homemade cart, Mr. Sharpe kept the potholes in our gravel road at bay. In the winter, a horse and sleigh helped to beat down the relentless snow just enough to make it passable when drifts sometimes nearly covered our little homes.

Once you gratefully and breathlessly reached the top of our hill, that one solitary, narrow dirt road extended approximately three kilometres. That area pretty much encompassed what was strictly known as Paradise back in the nineteenth century, right up until massive development commenced in the 1970s.

In addition to the entrance off Topsail Road, there was also another old dirt road at the other end of Paradise Road, which led up from the St. Thomas Line (known to locals as the Horse Cove Line) and St. Philips. There was a very tight link between us and the St. Philips area, and most families knew each other. Children would marry, become lifelong friends and acquaintances, or, on the odd occasion, become enemies.

Yes, we were a relatively small but vibrant collection of people back then. You knew everyone and were probably related to half of them. But believe me when I say that it was a wonderfully close-knit family community with a healthy and industrious heartbeat that was all its own.

There were only a handful of families nestled in and around that gravel road then, mostly having come in from Conception Bay and the surrounding areas. But those people met each morning very enthusiastically, lived active lives, and produced countless children, many of whom still live there today. I am one of those children. My father moved to Paradise as a boy with his family in the mid 1930s, but my lovely mother was already there. She was a born and bred resident of Paradise.

If you can identify any of the following names, you can more than likely recall some of the memories I'm going to share with you in the following pages. The prominent names in Paradise were and still are: McCarthy, Janes, Lynch, Coombes, Clark, Sharpe, Sears, Parsons, Rixon, Drover, English, Newman, Gosse, Murphy, Hussey and, of course, Pennell.

According to the census of 1921, there are older residents who moved to Paradise early in their lives but were not born there. It appears that the oldest family who was actually born and raised in Paradise is the McCarthy family. Richard McCarthy was born right in Paradise in October of 1871, as was his wife, Frances (no maiden name given). By 1921, they had three sons: Cyril, aged nine, William, aged seven, and Richard, aged four.

However, it's obvious that by 1921, Paradise was in full swing as a working community. There were twenty-three households according to the census, but my father and step-grandfather Rixon had yet to arrive. However, many of the family names listed above were well established there by then and had rapidly growing families. It would be approximately another fifteen years before my family cleared land and set up house in the area.

My maternal great-grandparents were the Janes family, one of the first to settle in Paradise from Upper Island Cove in what is now called Conception Bay North. Paradise was actually known as Woodville back then, and as the name indicates, it was heavily wooded. The first settlers had their hands more than full, considering they had to clear the land before the first nail was struck.

Turning right halfway along Paradise Road, you will notice that there is still a road named Woodville. Paradise was quite the isolated area then, with woods and meadows galore, but it held great promise for the first families who needed a chance for a fresh start and land to build a home on.

My father, Walter Pennell, entered this world in August of 1920. He was born to Herbert and Jessie (Lynch) Pennell, right at the top of Leslie Street, bordering on Hamilton Avenue, in St. John's West. That two-story house is still standing today, and I often drive by and think of my grandparents and my dad living there back when the twentieth century was still new.

Jessie Lynch was originally from Upper Island Cove. Herbert's father, Thomas Pennell, was a townie and so was his father, Thomas Sr. At the time of Thomas Jr.'s marriage to Sarah (known as 'Sadie' Rogers), his address was 77 Casey's Lane, which is now, of course, Casey Street just off LeMarchant Road. That house still stands and is located at the intersection of Casey Street and Brazil St. in downtown St. John's. Thomas Jr. and Sadie would become my great-grandparents.

Shortly after my father, Walter, was born, Herbert and Jessie relocated to 85 Pleasant Street in the downtown core, just off New Gower and Springdale Streets. The census of 1921 for St. John's registers many people at that address: Herbert and Jessie, my grandparents; Sadie, who was Herbert's mother; my father; his sister, Vera; and a brother, Herbert Jr., who died in 1923, aged two years, from measles. Another brother to Dad was Locklyn, who died in May of 1924, aged six months, with the cause of death simply listed as "not thriving."

That year, my grandfather, Herbert, succumbed to tuberculosis at the tender age of twenty-seven years. What a desperately sad and stressful period it surely had to be for my grandmother Jessie, losing two sons and her husband within a couple of years! My great-grandmother Sadie also had to endure the heart-wrenching experience of witnessing her son and grandsons fade away and eventually die.

Countless families suffered the loss of loved ones to that dreaded disease between the 1920s and 1940s. Tuberculosis has had several names throughout the ages, firstly known throughout Europe as the "white plague," and in the nineteenth century it was often referred to in death registers as 'consumption' and lastly simply "TB," which was the abbreviation of the dreaded word, tuberculosis. It has been a scourge since the early seventeenth century, with causes being attributed to witches, fairies, and, more accurately, to poor diet and poor air quality.

According to Heritage Newfoundland and Labrador, in the first fifty years of the twentieth century, no less than thirty-two thousand Newfoundlanders died of this highly contagious disease, most of whom were men between the ages of fifteen and forty-five. In other words, most households were now placed in the scary and insecure position of having to compensate for the loss of a father and/or brother who was, most assuredly, that household's breadwinner.

One of the reasons given for the high percentage of death was the fact that because of the long and frigid winters, most families in Newfoundland gathered in one spot, which, of course, would be the warm, inviting kitchen. Therefore, if one family member was unfortunate enough to contract tuberculosis, it was rapidly passed onto other family members because of their proximity.

Cod liver oil could be found in every medicine chest on the island around that time, as scientists had discovered that it assisted in the cure and prevention of this enduring white plague. Coffins being carried from houses almost daily was an all too common and threatening sight.

Grandmother Jessie Pennell, widowed at an early age because of TB, was a single parent responsible for her two children's welfare. Being the resilient fighter she always was, perseverance took control, and she carried on alone. Through that undaunted courage, she found work.

She quickly acquired a position in downtown St. John's at the popular Crosbie Hotel on Duckworth Street, where she was employed as a maid and housekeeper.

The Crosbie Hotel on Duckworth St. in St. John's,
Grandmother Jessie Rixon's first Employer.

She proudly reminisced as she spoke to me of having to line up each morning, usually outside on the sidewalk if the weather was fit, with other employees for inspection, as the cleanliness and neatness of uniforms were mandatory. Grandmother was quick to add, however, that she always passed that test.

Eventually, Grandmother Jessie met and married a hard-working and kind gentleman, Jim Rixon of Job's Cove in northwest Conception Bay, where she relocated with her children, Walter and Vera. Not having met my biological grandfather, as a child, I always considered Jim Rixon to be my actual biological grandfather. As children, we were never told the difference, but Grandfather Jim could not have been more beloved and revered, biological or not.

Growing up, my siblings and I were not aware of, nor did we ever think to ask, why our father's surname was Pennell and his "father's" surname was Rixon. As previously mentioned, we were too young to remember our natural grandfather. But let it be said that if ever there was a wonderful grandfather in every possible way, it was Jim

Rixon. He treated each of us as if we were his natural grandchildren and nurtured us daily.

Grandfather Jim Rixon, Dad's stepfather.

Personally, I have countless fond memories of spending pleasant hours with this kind man. He often sat at our table in our cozy kitchen, where he became a welcomed fixture. He regaled and entertained my siblings and me with amusing tales, some scary, about coming of age in Job's Cove in Conception Bay.

I can see him perfectly now, walking through the back wooded lane, approaching our house in all kinds of weather as he dangled his mug on his finger. Grandfather always knew there would be a pot of some kind of steaming hot and delicious soup, stew, or Sunday dinner on our stove. And, if he came late in the day when all had eaten, he would eagerly dip that mug into the boiler for a drop of "pot liquor," as he called it. In Newfoundland, the remaining liquid after all the meat and vegetables have been eaten is called pot liquor.

My mother treated him royally and always ensured that he was comfortable and fed. Jim Rixon was certainly a welcome addition to our house at any time. We were fortunate, and indeed blessed, to have had that smiling gentleman in our lives.

After my grandparents married and their blended families expanded, they relocated by about ten kilometres, from Job's Cove to Ochre Pit Cove. But around 1934, they eventually resettled closer to St. John's, in Paradise, when my father, Walter, was approximately fourteen years of age. The children at that time were Dad; his full sister, Vera; his half-sister, Jessie; his half-brother, Jim Jr.; and Grandfather's children from a previous marriage, Doug and Annie.

Left: Arch Locke and Annie (Rixon) Parsons. Annie was Dad's stepsister.

Right: Uncle Jim Rixon (Dad's half-brother) with his daughter, Mildred. Behind is a gravelled-road Paradise, fully wooded on the other side.

They were about to settle in a place where they would never leave, and Paradise itself would start its growth. Within the next ten years, a new generation would be quickly arriving. Soon, the name Pennell would be a familiar one in the Paradise area.

Setting Down Roots
in Paradise

Dad's biological father, Herbert Pennell, luckily had bequeathed land to him in Woodville, which was eventually renamed Paradise, on what we always referred to as Pennywell Road. If you were to look at a map of present-day St. John's, you could see how closely connected the Pennywell Road in St. John's intersects with our Pennywell Road if you just keep travelling west from St. John's.

My father and his stepfather, Jim Rixon, having made their way in from Conception Bay to this newly bequeathed land, were hoping and willing to work hard toward a more prosperous life. When Dad reminisced, he often went back to that time when he and his stepfather first walked on that land and talked about building. They started with a small, cozy bungalow right on that plot of land on Pennywell Road. Unfortunately, this land was inaccessible by road at the time, so, being innovative and logical, they uprooted the little bungalow and painstakingly towed it to the main road. It was then placed on newly acquired land, which Grandfather Rixon bought from a local and colourful character named Joey Lynch.

Mr. Lynch was fondly known in Paradise when I was a boy as Joey Roundboy. I will talk about Joey later, but for now, just know that he was the thinnest man I ever encountered.

It really pleases me to say that unbelievably that tiny, sweet bungalow is still standing today, and for all intents and purposes, it is relatively the same, apart from some minor renovations. It's also a happy thought that this minute structure is still occupied to this day by a member of the Rixon family. Ken Rixon, a second cousin, has lived and raised a family on the same spot as his Grandfather Rixon did.

This is the first little structure built by our family, more specifically by Grandfather Rixon when they first arrived in Paradise in the 1940s.

Even today when I pass it, I can vividly envision my grandparents out and about their house, feeding and talking to the chickens, Grandmother Jessie at the clothesline, or Grandfather bringing in an armful of wood for the stove. It was a welcome sight that I thought would never end and I'm grateful for the memory of it.

So, it's 1934, and the Rixon/Pennell family is now established and settled in their new abode in Paradise. What a wonderfully new beginning it must have been for Grandmother (Pennell) Rixon. She had started off her life in Lower Island Cove in Conception Bay, had come to St. John's to find work, and met her first husband, Herbert Pennell. As mentioned earlier, after having her growing Pennell family well underway in St. John's, she sadly lost her husband and several of their children.

Sometime later, she met Jim Rixon, they were married, and they moved to Ochre Pit Cove, not far from her birthplace. There, they started their own family but finally relocated to Paradise, not far from St. John's, where she had originally lived as a married woman to my natural grandfather, Herbert. With all the sickness on the island back in those early days, she kept her remaining children together and worked diligently to give them a wholesome home life.

Dad's stepfather, now permanently settled and working all the hours God kindly bestowed upon him, had the presence of mind to purchase enough land for all his children, Jim Jr., Doug, Jessie, and Annie, and he included his stepchildren, Walter and Vera, in that purchase. How fortunate they all were to have that kind of leg-up for when they matured themselves, contemplated marriage, and started a family of their own. It gives you an idea into the kind of foresight that Grandfather Rixon possessed.

That parcel of land extended from Flint Hill, coming into Paradise Road for approximately a kilometre, to the place where my family homestead stood. We were right on the doorstep of our school, which was built on land that Joey Lynch had kindly bestowed on the community.

When my father was about eighteen years old, he was more than anxious to start constructing his own family home. I remember him telling me how, without the luxury of a car or other transportation, he quite often stacked as many pieces of lumber as he could for our new home on the handlebars of his bicycle. He obviously had to make multiple trips, but it was a means toward an end, and that's how he accomplished it when he decided to build. Now that's what I call a will of iron, and that was his personality. He was quiet, kind-hearted, and rarely spoke unless something needed to be said. I remember being a very young boy, following him around while he worked on a project. He always showed me how it was done and ensured that I understood. He was never given to much conversation otherwise, but I never felt safer than I did when I had him close to me. He was an industrious individual, and I loved him dearly.

His days of courting had begun, and Walter knew that it wouldn't be long before he'd be starting his own family. And boy, did he start a family! Actually, the Pennell Family seemed to never stop growing. Before it was all said and done, there would be seventeen new Pennells in the world.

Not quite properly in order of age, I'll list them. Florie (my mother) and Walter's first-born was Herb, who was named after Dad's biological father. After that the flood gates opened, and there was a new baby in our household almost annually. Following Herb was Locklyn, me, Walter Jr. (Wally), Melvin (who unfortunately died as a child), Mac, Nelson, Jim, Florie, Joan, Lily, Ruby, Doreen, Jane and Janet (our twins), Michelle, and Brenda. How is that for "go forth and multiply," as the Bible says?

Me and my siblings:
Bottom Row: Michelle, Janet, Jane and Brenda
Second Row: Lilly, Florie, Ruby, Doreen
Third Row: Jim, Joan, Ches and Herb
Top Row: Nelson, Mac, Lock and Wally

I often wonder, in astonishment, at how many hundreds of loaves of bread our mother baked and how many diapers she put out on the line in the fresh Paradise air. I also wonder how much wood our father chopped and toted, and I marvel at how determined he was to find excellent-paying employment to responsibly raise that huge brood of his. Like most children, none of us really took the time to consider that, or else we were too young to appreciate the undying devotion both our parents obviously had for us. Luckily, and unlike so many others around us, we never went without anything we needed. Our parents made sure of that, and I will be eternally grateful to them both.

My mother arrived in this world, right in Paradise, as Florence (Florie) Parsons on January 15, 1925, to Maggie (Janes) and William (Billy) Parsons. The Janes family had been established in Paradise for decades, but the Parsons family had come from the south side of St. John's on what is now known as Shea Heights.

In my opinion, if you know my brother, Mac Pennell, you know what Grandfather Parsons looked like. History, or genetics, has repeated itself there. My maternal grandfather, known affectionately as Billy to most, was a farmer as well as a butcher, and he laboured as many hours as that implies. He certainly could never have been described as a lazy man. He worked on and around his property from the first crow of the rooster to whenever the sun set.

Florie, having probably inherited her work ethic from her father, was without the slightest doubt the hardest-working individual, either male or female, that I have ever witnessed in my entire life. Indeed, it was overall an environment of labour-intensive work for most people back then, day in and day out. But more importantly, their labours were carried out to support the daily lives of family, which was the pulse of the place and unconditional love for each other that kept it all functioning like a well-oiled machine.

My parents met at quite a young age, courted, were married, and became parents before Mom turned twenty. Only recently, I learned that it was Mr. Mose Gosse, who lived at the bottom of Flint Hill on Topsail Road, who drove them on their wedding day, as Mose was one of very few who owned a vehicle. He was a schoolteacher, an expert on window making who operated his own sawmill, and a talented artist as well.

It was only a year or so later that the little house, which Dad built himself after many trips on his bicycle from Chester Dawe Limited, welcomed their first-born, Herbert. From then on, the new Pennell homestead would be filled, year after year, with the sound of new-borns and laughter from many of their children.

Paradise
Sixty Years Ago!

When I let myself reminisce about being a young boy, outside playing or tackling one of my chores in the winter around dusk, I can easily wander back mentally to how peaceful and serene it all appeared to me. Nighttime in Paradise in the 1940s and 1950s could be compared to a heart-warming Norman Rockwell Christmas card. When I reflect back to my childhood, that's exactly what I envision. Walking along the dirt roads in the pitch black, it was so very quiet. All you would hear was the sound of your own footsteps on the gravel or the hard snow and the occasional *moo* or *bah* from nearby farm animals. Traffic was nearly non-existent. I can recall having to carry water from the well some evenings. I would stop momentarily to carefully lay the buckets down and catch my breath, and I would look up happily at the multitude of glimmering stars and the moon shining down... just on Paradise, I thought!

You would see smoke curling from all the chimneys that had hard-working woodstoves churning out the heat in the kitchens, with free-standing kerosene lanterns in the frosty windows. There were also the lanterns with the reflector on the back, like a tin-foil pie plate, hung on the kitchen walls up out of harm's way. Electricity hadn't reached us yet, so our only source of light was these glittering lanterns, and our only source of heat was the woodstove. But, you know, we didn't miss the convenience of electricity a smidgeon. And in retrospect, I have to say that electricity, when it finally did make its debut up our little road, wasn't half as inviting or cozy.

Everybody's kitchen was toasty warm and inviting, and every house was a familiar one. Every child in Paradise knew which houses held the best prospects for a slice of homemade bread, a cookie, or piece of cake. Our house, I'm proud to say, was one of those houses for all the neighbourhood children.

Any individual encountered along the road back then was a familiar face who would speak to you, or at least give you a hearty nod. Even the horses would come to you if you called them, and we knew all their names, too. Cars were few and far between and seemed like such a luxury item; if you wanted to get somewhere, you walked—and we walked a lot—or you hitched a ride on a horse and cart.

There were several sawmills along Paradise Road, locally owned and operated, and it was a common sound to hear the daily buzz of these saws. Uncle Jim Rixon, my father's half-brother, was one of those sawmill owners. As boys, we often helped Uncle Jim in his mill. We always referred to the bigger logs as "sticks," and we would huff and puff under the weight of those trying to place them up on the big saw. They would then be run through into a rough cut of two-by-fours or two-by-eights by our uncle, and I always remember how cautious he was when young boys were helping. The next step was to run them through the planer to polish off the finished product. When Uncle Jim was given a large order, you could hear the high and low pitches of that saw all day until the work was complete.

Uncle Jim Rixon's garden with felled trees ready for the sawmill. Note the new Holy Innocents' Church in the foreground.

One of the typical mills found in Paradise.

You were taught to conserve whatever you could and to avoid waste, we swept and gathered up the sawdust and curly pieces of wood, which we called chaff. Uncle Jim also sold this by the bag for fifty cents to the butchers in St. John's and surrounding areas for their floors to try to prevent anyone from slipping. Nothing was wasted if you could make a dollar off it. It was recycling in its finest form!

Most residents of Paradise had a garden, which usually included crops as opposed to flowers. Those gardens always held a hearty supply of "organic" vegetables long before we even knew we were living "organically." An exception to that, however, was Aunt Mildred (Lynch) Rixon, Uncle Jim's wife, who had an absolutely stunning and plentiful flower garden with all varieties of colourful creations, which she maintained daily. You could tell that she was passionate about her horticultural display, where she spent many happy hours during the summer. Most residents didn't bother with flowers or actually have time for them, but nearly everyone would linger long enough to admire hers.

Aunt Mildred Rixon, always busy in her bountiful flower garden.

Little Mildred Rixon, Cecil Lynch, and Aunt Mildred in their garden.

It was a treat to watch all those blossoms flourish in such a vivid display of every colour. This lady definitely had a green thumb and loved her own botanical garden. Like anything or anyone who is nurtured and loved, it flourished year in and year out. Those flowers seemed nearly magical at a time when really all you ever saw grow were vegetables and hay for survival. Aunt Mildred offered a field of beauty to anyone who wanted to gaze upon it or inquire about what each blossom was called, and she was eager to explain. At the time, it seemed like an honour to see what she produced from that bit of earth.

As a child running around my neighbourhood, the familiar sounds would be the crow of the rooster, horses neighing, cows mooing, the bleating of sheep, the sawmill operating, hens cackling around the property and the hen houses, and mothers calling to and checking on their children. All of this, of course, provided us with not only daily entertainment (which it shouldn't have, as we frightened the hens and sometimes the sheep), but it also provided a steady supply of fresh and necessary food.

Coming in from the cold, especially on a brisk winter's night, you would be met with the smell of our Mom's home cooking. And as sure as the sun came up in the morning, you would fill your lungs with the best aroma in the world coming from our ever-reliable woodstove. That aroma, of course, would be homemade bread! In our house, bread was mixed and baked every day, and sometimes, if we were particularly hungry, Mom would knead another full pan in the evening. Florie Pennell always had a batch 'on the rise' and always had a brood of hungry children waiting to receive their steaming-hot slice of bread with butter and a generous serving of molasses. It was such a delicious treat, and I feel well blessed to say that we always had some on hand.

In our kitchen on old Paradise Road, there was a long table with benches on either side, and at any given time, you could find eight to ten youngsters sitting around and partaking in whatever meal Mom had put in front of them. And, make no mistake, all those youngsters might not have been Pennells. Quite honestly, if you walked in our house at mealtime, you were fed—plain and simple. It didn't matter to our sweet mother what your last name was! If you were in her house with her children, you were treated to whatever her children got.

It always makes me chuckle to think of my childhood friend, Archie Sharpe, who always requested in his stammering way that his slice of homemade bread have "molasses down below and the butter up below!" We never quite knew what that meant, but it didn't matter because he was always delighted with what Mom gave him. And that was her nature, generous of heart and always aware of those who may be hungry.

Many people I meet today remember my parents with great fondness, and some of them with great gratitude, because some people in Paradise were legitimately hungry and didn't have what we had. There was always a steaming boiler of homemade soup, stew, pea soup or Sunday dinner simmering on our woodstove, and every person, young or old, had an invitation to "sit in," as she would say.

*My brother, Wally, with Mom and Arch Metcalf at our back door.
It was always open to neighbours.*

One of my favourite dishes was when Dad would wrap fish in a brown paper bag, lay it on hot, red embers in the woodstove, and turn it periodically. It cooked quickly and tasted as mouth-watering as any smoked fish you could order in a high-end restaurant today.

I always thought we had plenty of everything, but even if we didn't, I'm sure my parents would have shared whatever they actually did have with relatives and neighbours alike.

There were occasions when the weather, mostly snowstorms, wreaked havoc on residents travelling on foot, who lived further down Paradise Road. Every winter, people would come to our house to get out of the stormy weather, just to warm up with a cup of tea and something to eat, and then proceed on their way. However, there were also many occasions when, as a child, I would come out in the morning and find one, two or even three people lying asleep by the stove, wrapped in one of Mom's quilts because they were unable to make the extra distance in the snow. Of course, she wouldn't hear tell of them going out when, "you couldn't see a hand before you." They were invited to stay, were well fed, and were given a safe haven to lie down in warmth and comfort until the storm subsided.

There was also a humorous occasion when a male stranger came to the door in the winter. I don't recall if there was a storm at the time. The poor man looked tired and inadequately dressed for the weather. He said that he had walked a long way and was looking for a family who lived much further down the road heading toward St. Philips. Mom, of course, opened the door, invited him in, and sat him down to a cup of tea and a bite to eat. She also filled up a glass jar with tea and put it in a sock to keep it warm for him when he left. He thanked her and was on his way.

It turned out that he had escaped from the Waterford Hospital (which was always referred to as "The Mental" by all of Newfoundland) that very same day. Well, Mom, of course, was unaware of that fact, and even when she was made aware of it later, her thought was that he could get just as hungry as any other person. She didn't react, and she didn't judge; she just did what she did best, and that was to be hospitable to anyone civil who stepped over her doorstep.

Now, having said that, though, if you were inclined to be an argumentative individual or clearly had one "swally" too many, she would address that problem immediately and without mincing her words. You were ordered to leave and not return if that was how you presented yourself. You toed the line and behaved, or you would experience the wrath of Florie Pennell's fury, which, speaking from experience as a sometimes-misbehaving child, is not a place anyone would want to be. Her displeasure produced a fierce look that nobody wanted to experience. She was no pushover, and that's for sure, but you always knew where you stood with her.

I recall that there were three brothers, George, Raymond, and Roland Clark, who often stopped by the house on their way to do some cutting in the woods. Even though they repeatedly and cordially told Mom that they didn't need a lunch, a thermos, or a bottle of tea for the day, she always insisted that they take a loaf of bread and something to make a sandwich with, plus a hot drink. Maybe that's why they stopped by.

I can see her now as she'd carefully put all the makings of a decent lunch in a metal pot with a handle as tidy as she could make it. And she'd say, "drop that pot back now on the way home." After hours of chopping and lugging, the boys made their way home. Of course, they did as she said and dropped in with the empty pot, and they were always very grateful to her for those lunches.

I guess that Mom assumed that being growing boys, they just had to be hungry again. Next thing, they would put the empty pot on the counter, sit in as she requested, and get a cup of pot liquor or a bowl of soup with some bread. Such was my mother. There was no pomp and circumstance, no formalities, but always an invitation to come in, sit down, and enjoy a bowl of something nourishing. I can't remember her ever being otherwise.

Speaking of our lovely old woodstove reminds me of the Saturday night bath time ritual in our house. I don't think many people on the whole of the island had showers back then, and it certainly wasn't the custom to bathe daily, other than a quick wash of the hands and face. Sometimes you washed your neck if your mother happened by and she observed. Then it was out the door to school.

On each and every Saturday night, without fail, once supper was all squared away and dishes done, the kerosene lamps would be lit, a dozen towels and pairs of long johns and pyjamas (matching or not) would appear, and dear old Mom would pull out a twenty-gallon GSW galvanized tub smack dab in the middle of our kitchen floor accompanied by a long, bright yellow bar of Sunlight soap. Who could forget the look and smell of it?

You wouldn't find any particular brand of shampoo or conditioner for dry or damaged hair back then. No, sir! It was the old reliable "good for any type of dirt," in or out, Sunlight soap. That stuff was even shaved off the bar and put in poultices for infections... Talk about multi-purpose products! I don't know if it was the soap in those poultices our parents concocted, but they always seemed to work.

Rain or shine on Saturdays, Mom would have water filled to the top in the warmer on the old woodstove. Once that was hot enough, she would add it to the room-temperature water she had already poured in this gigantic tub. When that was done, her sleeves rolled up and with Sunlight soap in hand, Florie Pennell was as equipped as any drill sergeant and ready to bathe her brood.

There would be all assortments of naked Pennells running around happily in the dimly lit, toasty warm kitchen, awaiting their turn in the comforting, soapy tub. The boys would step in the tub first, anxious to splash their brothers. To this day, I can still feel the vigorous, head-to-toe scrubbing that Mom gave us as every inch was made squeaky clean. Then you would be on the receiving end of a couple of pots of warm water poured over your head as a rinse. If you weren't quite ready for that, you could be spewing bath water with the unforgettable taste of good old Sunlight soap all night. It was no gentle spa with nature sounds piped in the background, but you could be assured that you came out clean.

Once Mom was satisfied that there was no dirt and everyone's hair and scalp was scrubbed, out we got. Quickly wrapped in a towel, we stood back on and front on to the stove until we felt sufficiently dry. You'd then scurry to pull on a pair of pyjamas or long johns. It really didn't matter whose if they fit. We then proceeded to make ourselves busy looking for a little mischief, because then it was some of the girls' turns.

If the water had cooled off, she would issue a warning to all children within a ten-foot radius to "keep clear," as she slowly carried the full dipper of scalding hot water from the stove's warmer across the floor to the huge tub before the next instalment of children stepped in it. Stirring the water sufficiently and getting her second wind as she paused to push back the hair away from her face with her arm, Mom would lather up, grab a little body, and resume her scrubbing.

There would be so much chatter, laughter, playing, whining over the scrubbing, and splashing that it was amazing that we all actually got bathed. But bathed we were because there was zero chance of avoiding it. My poor, hard-working mother would be soaked to the skin, but she never seemed to notice or complain.

Privacy wasn't an issue at that age, but fun was, and we had that in abundance. With the baby bathed last (and hopefully not thrown out with the bath water), the galvanized tub was emptied, pot by pot, until it got light enough for a couple of the boys to lift it out the back door to throw the water out. A week's worth of good Paradise dirt gone... until next Saturday night, when the whole procedure was repeated.

It's funny how, as kids, we didn't stop to think of the time and immense effort those Saturday night baths for six or eight children at any given time, took on our mother's part. Only as you age do you realize, appreciate, and thank God for how cared for you were and how good you actually had it! Overall, I'm proud to say that my parents were big-hearted and selfless people who laboured daily, put family first and foremost, and treated people equally.

The Pennell house, though sturdily built, wasn't a grand structure. But it was adequate for what we needed and was never short on love and protection. It was, without a doubt, that kind of friendly home where people regularly gathered and felt welcome to do so, and that is the most precious memory I gently take with me from my childhood in Paradise.

Mr brother, Mac, with Mom and Dad in our living room.

An Enterprising
Man Named Walter

My father, Walter Pennell, was quite the skilled carpenter by trade. He also worked for the Americans during and after World War II at Fort Pepperrell in St. John's, at Harmon Air Force Base in Stephenville, and in Argentia, which is on the southwest coast of the Avalon Peninsula.

Dad, as anyone who knew him would attest, was one of the most reserved—but most innovative—individuals ever witnessed. Quite frequently, he brought home ideas from those bases, and our family would always benefit from them.

I remember following him around as a youngster, with a hammer or screwdriver, eagerly trying to be his assistant. Dad would always permit me to be that assistant. He was a wonderful teacher indeed, and he would take the time to instruct me about what needed to be done and then demonstrate how to do it. Whenever I hear country artist, Tim McGraw's current song "Humble and Kind", I think of him.

On one particular occasion, I vividly recall Dad coming in our back door to the kitchen and promptly stating that we wouldn't be using the outhouse any longer. He had seen how a bathroom was plumbed "on the Base." He then endeavoured to devise, construct, and install one of the very first indoor toilets in Paradise.

It amazed me how our father always went about his projects very quietly and ambitiously, but obviously confidently, because the end result always seemed to work out to his well-deserved satisfaction.

As if it were yesterday, I can recollect mixing the concrete by hand and picking up bigger rocks to put in the forms to construct an eight-by-eight septic tank. The pipes were three and four feet long, which extended from the septic tank at the back of the house, and covered an area of approximately one hundred feet, where it reached the new bathroom off the kitchen area.

We were now the proud owners of a toilet and stationery bathtub. No more dragging out the huge, galvanized tub for Mom to fill with water from the heater on the woodstove. And we boys were now off the hook to empty that tub every Saturday night. We were happily dumbfounded! In our minds, Walter Pennell could do and build anything. And, of course, Dad—and his improvements—didn't stop there!

On the side of our woodstove was a four- or five-gallon warmer, the one that had previously aided with the Saturday night bathing ritual. Dad decided to hook up our very first hot water boiler so there would always be a steady supply of hot water.

Ted Sharpe, one of our neighbours, was a plumber. He and my father got a glass-lined tank that was seven feet tall and twelve inches on the round and placed it directly behind the woodstove. They concocted a system where they ran copper pipes from the stove to the tank, which then heated the water as it went into the tank. Up to that point, we didn't have hot, running water coming out of a faucet, but through his ingenuity, now we did. And we even had a new bathtub with a hot water faucet. I proudly thought to myself that, make no mistake, we had to be the most modern family in Paradise and beyond. Hot water at any time seemed nearly magical!

When Newfoundland Light and Power cut a pole line down through Paradise in 1952, my father's next project was introducing electricity into our house. Up to that point, our little community's only source of light was candles and lamps, and electricity didn't seem important.

With his old tools at the ready, Dad installed the reliable knob and tube method. Now the Pennell family had modern electricity, and I can still feel the excitement of the first night we experienced it. That evening was thrilling! We thought it was a wonderfully progressive thing then, even if it seemed awfully bright. It was a wonder to me, though, just having to flick a switch to spontaneously light up our little bungalow.

The whole concept was a little daunting but incredibly modern to a young child who didn't understand how it all happened. I can remember Mom stating that she never realized what a lovely home we had until the lights demonstrated it in full colour.

Initially, whenever our parents weren't in the same room as us, we would mischievously take turns switching the lights off and on. Of course, within a minute, we got caught and ordered to stop. It was indeed a novelty, but like all novelties, we got used to it.

Yes, it was certainly progressive and convenient, yet the memories of the flickering kerosene lamps still feel much warmer than anything electricity could ever have produced. I loved those old lamps and still have them to this day. I light them periodically, as they bring back a swarm of good memories—not to mention that they're still as attractive as they were when I was a child!

Convenience was a definite plus, but to my mind, some of the cozy and intimate atmosphere of the home was lost when electricity was introduced. To me, it seemed stark and intrusive, but obviously it served a good purpose, and after a while, I was happy to have it.

At that time, cars were regarded as a real luxury item, and few residents were fortunate enough to own one. My father was the type of individual who never demanded much out of life, but he absolutely loved to have a nice vehicle. However, there was a problem: he wouldn't ever buy a new one. I guess he thought that it would be a waste of his hard-earned money when he possessed the ability to put a good car together himself. And that was a true fact. There was also the fact that he enjoyed the challenge. It was similar to a giant jigsaw puzzle to him.

He paid a visit to Dodge City, one of our local car dealerships, which was (and still is) on Topsail Road, and bought a 1956 Dodge for the princely sum of fifty dollars. The fact that there was no engine in this Dodge didn't seem to perturb him a whole lot. He knew where there was a 1955 Dodge which had been sideswiped at some point, and it was also selling for fifty dollars. This one, luckily, had a wonderful six-cylinder engine. I was with him when he bought this vehicle and brought it home. It was a Friday night, I remember specifically. If anyone other than Dad had bought these cars, I would have been quite skeptical about either one of them ever seeing the road again.

Neither one of those vehicles sat idle for long. On Saturday morning, I worked enthusiastically alongside him as he took that beauty of an engine out of the 1955 and put it in the 1956. Then he studied all eight tires and picked the best four, which I helped him replace. We cleaned up our "new" car, adding a dab of paint here and there and smoothing out the odd dent. That Sunday night, I turned the ignition and drove Mom and Dad to Bingo in it.

Dad didn't think it any great accomplishment to do that, and he was certainly never one to pat himself too heartily on the back. It was just sensible and feasible to do it that way. There were many men then—and many men today—who couldn't handle a project like that. But if Dad had a plan, he worked it. Whether by luck or nature, he possessed a real understanding of mechanisms.

There was never much discussion about any project, but there was always a great deal of thought. And what happened to the 1955 Dodge which he got the engine from, you may ask? He sold it to Vatcher's Used Auto Parts on Thorburn Road for scrap, of course. So, for less than a mere hundred dollars, we were stylishly mobile.

If any of our cars ever needed a paint job, Walter would do that too, and it really makes me chuckle to think of the process he devised to carry that out. He would either buy paint from the Royal Garage or mix his own from leftovers he had. Let it be said that he came up with some really interesting, yet pleasant colours.

The car would be sanded down, and he would use Polybond on some of the more difficult spots. The area to be painted would then be taped off. Next, he would take an old vacuum cleaner. Mom had upgraded to a bigger and better model, but the old one was going to be quickly recycled and put to good use.

This vacuum was a little green Electrolux shaped just like an egg, and it had been our very first one. From the exhaust hose on this vacuum, he would hook on or tape on the top of the bottle of paint, which he had just mixed. Placing a finger or two over the exhaust hole on the top of the bottle, the vacuum cleaner would be turned on, and he could manipulate how much paint was actually spraying out. As soon as he got the flow of the spray just right by experimenting on old scrap metal lying nearby, he quickly directed the flow toward the car, and pronto! It received a new paint job. It was as easy as that. I had never seen that done before, and I haven't seen it done since. I can't say that I ever attempted to do that myself, because to me, it looked like a disaster waiting to happen. You had to possess quite the steady hand. But for Dad, the car would look like it just came off the showroom floor. It was a joy to watch him work.

In smaller communities like Paradise, there was usually one or two men who mended shoes. You would never see a female doing that because they had their jobs, and the men had theirs. Shoemaking was definitely a male assignment. Dad was one of the town's recognized cobblers, and his ability to fix boots and shoes was always in demand. A Last , which is a metal replica of a foot, placed upside down, was the tool he used. The footwear to be fixed was fitted onto the Last and the hammering and mending was done while it was held in place...

A foot last like the one Dad used for repairing our shoes and boots.

The pieces of leather that were brought home were cut and shaped to fix our shoes. Working on the various bases, Walter would periodically buy or acquire new, and some not-so-new, cadet-type boots that were being sold off. We would all sit around the kitchen, try them on, and then pick a pair. If they needed work, he would put his cobbler skills to the test, and then you were the owner of a new pair of boots. With eight or ten energetic children in the house at any given time, going and growing by the day, he was kept busy on his Last.

Our father was certainly busy enough fitting and fixing his children's newly acquired footwear, but the locals would bring their shoes and gaiters to the house for him to revive as well.

I remember having a pair of gaiters mended only to tear a hole in them the very next day while I was out sliding. I thought that I would get away with it because there were always so many pairs of footwear in our back porch. But nothing escaped Mom's eagle eye, and she found it the first night after I thought that I had so carefully buried my pair. Not much was said, certainly not by Dad, and he just took the ripped gaiter and got out his trusty old Last. It's no wonder that we didn't (and still don't) understand the concept of being bored. Who had the time for it? Not Dad, for sure!

Honestly, I don't think there was a day that Dad arrived home without bringing back something from those military bases. Whether it was an idea for a project, food, footwear, or anything else we could possibly use, he always brought something home.

At times, there would be soldiers pulling up in the driveway, with Dad at the wheel. He would sometimes give them a lift to town for a few days' leave. They always seemed to have lots of chocolate, which we were happy to take off their hands, along with cigarettes for the adults. Sometimes, you'd be lucky enough to acquire a mouth organ from them, and you would spend the rest of the evening trying to manage it. Some of those soldiers were quite skilled at playing those instruments, and you would readily recognize a melody from the radio.

I thoroughly enjoyed talking to a soldier or two as they waited in our kitchen for Dad to load up his passengers and get back on the road to Argentia. One young fellow, I remember, had celebrated a little too much on his leave and had no money left for his passage out. So, he gave Dad his watch, which was the standard type issued to all military. That watch was passed on to me. I have never worn it, as I consider it a keepsake from that time period and my father. But I do take it out from time to time when I reminisce about those days at home and those young soldiers telling me about their hometown and their families. I probably helped ward off a little of their homesickness.

How I wish those days were recorded on video! What seemed like a normal, uneventful day back then would now be regarded as being absolutely priceless. Time is a wonderful teacher.

With quite a keen eye and more than his share of common sense prevailing, my father could mechanically engineer anything. Once he saw something done or observed how a mechanism operated, he could replicate it easily. I somehow thought that all men must be like that, but as I got older, I realized that this wasn't the case. I'm delighted to state that he has passed that gift on to some of my own sons, and as with Dad, it is always to the family's benefit.

Next in line on his "new and improved" list was our very first refrigerator. The only fridge I had seen at that point was in Mrs. Gosse's General Store; it was full of polar bars, popsicles, and Dixie Cups. Gosse's was on Topsail Road, just down over Flint Hill leading up to Paradise. Until then, our young minds didn't consider refrigeration as a domestic necessity, simply because we had always functioned without it. We assumed that they were only necessary in shops and stores.

There were, of course, root cellars, which were quite common in our neck of woods for storing various vegetables over the winter. But generally, people just acquired meats and fish on a regular basis for consumption.

Our first fridge was very typical of the 1950s' version. It was about four feet tall, with rounded corners and a long handle, which had to be pulled down to open. The only problem was that we had precious little space in our kitchen for such a big appliance. All of us children took up a fair amount of floor space, for one thing. But that was no problem for Walter!

I can see him now, sizing up the situation and the dimensions. He decided to cut a hole in the kitchen wall over the basement stairs and then proceeded to build a box-like container, which protruded over the stairs. This structure wasn't so big that you couldn't navigate up and down the staircase, however. Then, into this container, the fridge was placed.

Entering the kitchen, all you saw of this newly acquired appliance was its front door. That was very innovative for the time. We kept hens' eggs, fresh meat, and fresh milk from Aunt Marion Lynch's cow in there, along with various vegetables from the garden. We thought we were the most modern people in Newfoundland, let alone Paradise. If the local magazine, *The Newfoundland Herald,* had been on the go back then, I would've suggested that my father should have been on the cover as The Most Ingenious Newfoundlander.

Years later, through Dad's efforts and a little help of some of us boys, our little three-bedroom bungalow, which he had built in the early 1940s, was significantly renovated to become a massive two-storey house. Dad would hear of a building closing or being torn down and off he would promptly go, looking for supplies for our extension. He was usually interested in radiators, but you would never know what was going to arrive home in the back of his car.

One time, he and Mom heard of such a building on Bell Island, which is located not far from us in Conception Bay. Off they went the very next day in Dad's old reliable station wagon to catch the ferry down in Portugal Cove. Later that evening, they arrived home with the car weighed down nearly to the gravel road. In the back were three or four huge and very heavy radiators, which I struggled to help him carry inside. When he went to install those radiators, he engineered all the pipe work that was needed, and it was painstaking, laborious work for sure. But the price was right, and when all was said and done, they churned out heat beautifully in our big house.

Our newly renovated house was jokingly referred to by the family as The Bog Hotel, simply because we lived directly across from a bog, but mostly because the sheer size of it said 'hotel' . It certainly wasn't too big, however, because our family (and by then extended family) could quite sufficiently fill it.

My sister, Joan Lawlor, with Mom, giving the newly renovated 'Bog Hotel' a fresh coat of paint.

Many of my siblings lived here periodically when they were first married. Most of the family's wedding receptions were held at our new and improved house, and they were catered by Mom, of course, who worked for days to feed one and all. As the expression goes, she served everything from soup to nuts, with a beautifully decorated wedding fruit cake sitting ceremoniously in the middle of the table for the new bride and groom.

Unfortunately, some years after adding that big extension, our father was taken ill. He developed a tumour on the brain, which rendered him totally unable to work. Devastating as that had to be for him, watching this dynamo of a man slow down and gradually become incapacitated was excruciating for us to witness. And as quiet an individual as he always had been, he became even more so.

The sad reality was that Walter Pennell would never work another day in his life, nor would he be collecting another paycheque. All of this being said however, his overall demeanour was still unaffected. He was as gentlemanly as ever, but now he very rarely even spoke. Now, it was *our* turn to take care of *him*.

Dad with my sister, Florie Sanders, in 1979

The Table Turns,
But The Work Goes On

So, with half a dozen children still left at home to raise, Mom became the sole breadwinner. For most people, I think, this would have been a daunting task. But for Mom, it was just a matter of rolling your sleeves up a little higher and figuring out how to make it work for all concerned. That is clearly what resilience looks like! I don't think she ever entertained the concept of 'can't.' She consistently moved full steam ahead and was, honestly, an inspiration.

Looking back at my parents now, I fully realize what a fantastic couple they were. They worked together harmoniously, and both were confident and competent people. As docile a man as our father was, our mother was the absolute opposite. To say that she could be verbal with us would be an understatement. Yet, they consistently respected each other and appeared quite content and happy. That's quite the recipe to have for a married couple. If they had their quarrels and differences when we were growing up, we were never made aware. We were incredibly fortunate to have that consistent atmosphere in our daily lives, and we really didn't even fully realize it at the time.

With Dad now disabled, Mom had to find outside work, and find it she did. As hard as it may be to believe, there were times when in addition to the six or so children still left at home and sitting around our kitchen table, there were at time upwards of twenty boarders there too. It was fortunate that Dad built that extension when he did! Our house became well known as the place to stay for out-of-towners who were employed at the various businesses, such as the Birch Plant, McNamara's, or any business on or near Topsail Road.

Dad was now at home permanently but helped where he could and worked alongside Mom as she busied herself with everything that running a boarding house entailed. Men leaving for an eight-hour shift were packed a hearty lunch and came home to just as hearty a supper. Beds were stripped, bed sheets were constantly flying on the line out in the yard most months of the year, boilers were steaming on the stove, children were cared for, and a pan of rising bread was waiting to go in the stove day in and day out.

The older kids helped where they could with hanging out clothes, bringing in the same clothes; at times, they were frozen stiff in the February air, and we stood them up in the kitchen as they thawed. There were also ongoing tasks, like making up and stripping beds and peeling all the vegetables that were required daily. Mom wouldn't tolerate any laziness, and if the whole family, even the children, had to pitch in to make life work, then they were expected to do so. Complaints went unheard and were frowned upon.

There were rules and regulations as with any house, and boarders were expected to abide by them as well. For the boarders, any type of alcohol was forbidden inside the house, as was the presence of outside women upstairs in the rooms. Everyone and anyone was welcome in our kitchen, but that's as far as you got. Who could blame Mom and Dad for those rules? After all, there were still impressionable children there, and the house was congested enough with those who actually did live there.

To my memory, there was only one guest who was permitted to drink. This quiet man worked at the Birch Plant down on Topsail Road, but he was susceptible to kidney stones. He was advised by his doctor to drink beer daily to help flush these stones. I remember that he was permitted to do so, but only in his bedroom, and he wasn't to let other boarders see him drink. He observed the rules and caused no trouble, with or without the beer. Maybe he was lying through his teeth, but he paid his bill promptly and caused no trouble. I'm sure Mom probably suspected his story was a false one, but she seemed to trust him, and he didn't disappoint.

Coming into our house during that period was like visiting a barracks. There would always be a type of assembly line in the kitchen, as lunches were being put together for the night shift men or the table was being readied for the shift just finishing work and coming home to supper. Mom was never skimpy when it came to meals, and there was never a complaint received about that. She was so used to cooking for such a crowd all the time that I'm sure that having to throw in extra vegetables for boarders wasn't too much of a chore for her.

When payday at the various plants came, Florie would don her banker's hat, get out her strong box as she sat at the kitchen table, and take the boarders' rent as they came home. She changed their cheques, and each man received the proper change to the penny. Come Monday morning, off Mom would go to the bank with those cheques in hand. Personnel at the bank was aware of her business arrangements and those cheques would be deposited to her account. It was a great set-up convenience-wise—all our boarders were delighted that Mom had saved them a trip to the bank, and they had cash on hand immediately. It also worked for Mom, as she was paid her rent upfront.

She didn't fool around, our mother, but she got paid on time and she delivered her part of the bargain on time. Then all hands sat down to a delicious but simple meal she had prepared, and so it went week in and week out.

According to accounts I've heard over the years, if you needed a place to stay for work, our house would have received a five-star rating. When boarders had finished their time of employment and were ready to go home, they would recommend someone, maybe a relative, from their hometown who wanted to board with us. The vacancy sign never had to be hung.

In those later years, though, an "A for effort" should have been awarded to Mom and Dad for having the grit they both possessed for making The Bog Hotel a successful venture. Credit card companies today would frown upon that kind of determination, I'm sure. Everything was done on a cash basis. It was, by all accounts, a make or break situation, and they both buckled down, along with some assistance from their offspring. Outstandingly, they made it work.

Years later, when all the children were grown and Dad had passed away, the boys decided to make the house more liveable for our mother. So, the huge two-storey building was dismantled and reverted back to a small bungalow. Isn't it marvellous that most of us were qualified carpenters like Dad? When the project was finished, our little house was back again, just as it was when we were small. Now, Florie didn't have to work all those long hours, and neither did she have to clean and maintain that big house. It had resolved to her satisfaction, and she was happy.

The Family Grocers
Loved To See Us Coming

Years before the endeavour of extending our house became necessary, firstly to house all the family, and then for survival, Dad's paycheque came from the Americans, where he was employed at several of the military bases. And for the time, that paycheque was a substantial one. Of course, with a very large family to feed and a new baby being introduced pretty much annually, it was fortunate for us that the Americans did pay as well as they did. For our family, the military presence was indeed a blessing.

It's a sad commentary on those times, however, that many men drank the best portion of their paycheques and their families went without and suffered because of it. We had our share of heavy drinkers in Paradise, but alcohol abuse was a common occurrence all over Newfoundland.

Dad wasn't a drinker by any stretch of the imagination, and in my opinion, our family surely benefited by that. Moreover, I'm sure that the Americans benefited from having a competent carpenter and a responsible individual like Dad in their employ. He was fond of most of the American boys he met, and they appeared to respect him when they sat around our kitchen on the odd occasion. They all knew that Walter loved his smokes, though, and he was never short of them when the soldiers were around.

I loved Dad's paydays when I was small because I knew what it meant. It was a delightful sight to behold, after a payday, when our father and mother pulled into our gravel driveway in his old 1947 seven-passenger Dodge, which was dragging closer to the ground than usual. That poor, old, grey car would be blocked to the ceiling, and sometimes had packages tied to the roof, full of provisions for everyone in the house for the next couple of weeks.

An exact replica of Dad's famous 1947 seven-passenger Dodge.

The grandmother or aunt who was babysitting us wouldn't know what had happened when we, having seen them drive in our lane, would all spring up and make a mad dash out through the back door to happily bring the boxes of groceries in. Oh, the chatter was deafening and the excitement in the kitchen over those boxes was unbelievable!

On one autumn night, the first snowstorm of the year came earlier than usual. Mom and Dad were out and about with paycheque in hand, picking up supplies all around town, and they got caught in this blustery snow on their way home..

As Mom later reminisced about that day, she would say that she left around noon in sunny, mild weather, wearing her Sunday best dress and raglan, and returned home in the height of a winter storm, trudging through snow that was now up to her knees in her high heels. It's what most Newfoundlanders would call an "awful dirty night out!"

With all the weight of the provisions they had bought, the heavily ladened Dodge nearly, but not quite, made its way home. They were stuck with tires spinning on the bottom of Flint Hill, which was quite the climb on a summer's day, even in a vehicle. They then attempted to drive around to St. Thomas Line to avoid climbing the hill, which wasn't much better. So, turning around, they tried to get our old Dodge up that steep hill again. Dad hoped that the weight of all the boxes and crates of groceries would help their ascent. But it wasn't to be.

At that time, Paradise didn't receive any of the typical municipal services, such as water and sewer. More importantly, on this occasion, our road was never plowed during a storm either. That function was left to the residents with their shovels, or the horses and carts that beat down the accumulated snow so it was passable.

I remember that night well, and I remember feeling oddly worried and scared as we all took turns looking out the front window, hoping to catch a glimpse of their headlights in the falling, swirling snow. It was unusual for them to be so late, especially on grocery day, and the storm had turned really nasty by now.

It was then that a kindly neighbour, Elsie Clarke, who lived on Topsail Road at the bottom of the hill, saw and heard them slipping and sliding in the car. Looking out her kitchen window through the squalls, she recognized the car as Walt's and immediately told one of her sons to tackle up their horse and slide. That old horse, cart, and driver were a welcome sight when they came to my parents' rescue. My poor mother, dressed more for the summer than the winter, hopped on the cart, and with Dad's arms wrapped securely around her, she finally got up over that hill and home.

It felt like such a gratifying, if not surprising, sight for all us little ones crowding the front room window, chattering and speculating amongst ourselves about what could have possibly happened to them, to finally see the horse with his head bent down against the windy squalls. He trudged slowly down the snow-covered road and turned into our lane.

I felt immediate relief as I recognized, through the snowy gales, the people sitting on board as my parents, with Dad jumping off first and trying to shield a frozen Mom from the then blizzard. He reached up and helped her down, but unfortunately she stood in a drift in her stockings and high heels as we hurriedly and excitedly ran to meet her at the back door. I have never forgotten how small and vulnerable our mother appeared and how bitterly cold she was. She shivered for a long time on a kitchen chair in front of the woodstove with her hands wrapped around a cup of tea as we did our childish best to sufficiently revive her.

Dad wandered in through the back door, snow-covered and proceeded to stamp his feet in the porch. He had managed to take a couple of boxes of groceries with the help of Elsie Clarke's son, who was toting a generous load himself. They then went back out into the blinding snow to try and retrieve the rest.

The next morning, we rose bright and early and were greeted with a sunny, blue sky. When we got outside, it was amazing to see our little bungalow nearly totally buried on one side. Our main priority then was to start to shovel out, and all hands were ready and willing to go down over the hill to rescue Dad's old Dodge. The huge drifts didn't bother us a bit, even though some were taller than I was. We knew that the bottom line was that we managed to thaw out our poor rescued mother, we had plenty of food, and we were on our way to help our Dad, who was also safe and sound.

On fair weather days, however, any family members who were home when they slowly pulled in from their trip to St. John's would run at breakneck speed out of the back door of our house and pitch in to carry the most-welcomed bounty into the house.

Growing up in Paradise and the general area, every single resident was familiar with Soper's on Topsail Road, and we all loved to go there. For children and adults, the big draw would be their huge, all-white building, which housed their Fish and Chip Shop. People from far and wide around St. John's and Conception Bay would visit Soper's for exactly that attraction. That establishment fed a goodly portion of the populace back then, and they were one of the most popular establishments on the Avalon Peninsula.

Soper's also had a smaller building next to their Fish and Chip Shop, which housed a grocery and gas bar. You could buy the regular food staples of the day, such as butter, salt, and milk, and they also offered vegetables of all types from the farmers in the area.

When the spring of the year came, it was a common sight outside any grocer's door, as well as Mr. Soper's, to see a brace or two of rabbits hung at the entrance. Alongside the brace of furry rabbits, there would be ducks or turrs, which are migratory seabirds somewhat resembling a small penguin. You bought either one of the items and headed home to pluck and/or skin it.

Before supermarkets arrived, it was a happy and most welcome sight to see fresh meat after a long winter. However, some young girls going in the shop always made a bit of a fuss about how sad the rabbits' eyes looked. I don't think the grocers were feeling any significant grief about it, though, and the animals didn't have much of a choice! I'm also a little dubious about the local Department of Health's picky regulations nowadays, as all the grocers practised that display, and we all lived to tell the tale of eating those rabbits and birds. Sadly, you don't see that practice at all today on the Avalon.

W.J. Murphy's Grocery on the corner of Rawlin's Cross, right in the middle of St. John's, was our main grocer. Mr. Murphy sold everything a household would need, from every type of food to a variety of furnace oils, as well as that brace of rabbits hanging on his front door in the spring.

More stops would have to be made in and around the town for heavier bulk items, however. It took some effort and muscle to lug all those boxes and packages out of the shops into the car, and then out of the car into our house. But it was satisfying to get it all home and witness the youngest of the children standing in the kitchen and gaping at the wonder of it all, as if they had found treasure, just as I had some years before.

What a variety of groceries, barrels, and sacks there would be to place in our pantry, with all its shelves and cupboards. When it was full, you couldn't imagine it ever being empty again. But with our own personal version of *The Old Woman in the Shoe* under our roof, it quickly thinned out. I can gratefully say that I never saw it totally empty, and that's a testimony to my parents' organization.

Given my sweet tooth, I'm happy to report that Dad would also faithfully visit the various bakeries in and around St. John's and get several large sacks of "cheese-cuttings." I was often lucky enough to be one of the children selected for those excursions when we visited Mammy's Bakery and Our Own Bakery. Just the smell of these establishments would make you hungry, especially when you're a ten-year-old boy.

Cheese-cuttings! I have no idea why they were called that because there was no cheese in the bag. It was what some people called bags of "ends." They were the edges of trays of squares, cakes, and cookies, all thrown in this one big, wonderful variety bag. Oh, how we loved to see those huge, lovely cloth sacks come in over the doorstep!

All Paradise knew when Walter Pennell had visited the bakeries, and our kitchen would gradually fill up with hungry citizens looking for something sweet to eat. Of course, this was after all the Pennell brood had their share of them, which we always did—with a hearty appetite intact.

There was every conceivable type of cookie and cake in that sweet-smelling bag, and we sampled all of them. And when I say that it was a huge bag, I mean exactly that. It was a hundred-pound flour sack that was filled to the absolute brim. We were a fortunate lot because my father knew a man by the name of Charlie Antle at Mammy's Bakery on Alexander Street in downtown St. John's. Charlie was one of the managers there, and he knew full well that those cheese-cuttings, which would probably be thrown out, would go a long way in a house full of kids. He was always generous in the portions. What a delicious treat all those varied pieces and parts of cakes and cookies were! Best of all, I know that our industrious father had paid precious little for the lot. You haven't lived until you've stuck your hand down a hundred-pound flour sack and wondered what sweet delight you were going to pull up! Honestly, those cheese-cutting occasions, when I waited for my turn with all my siblings, are one precious memory.

Dad would also buy many cases of Jell-O. Every Saturday, Mom would open several packages of it to make for Sunday supper, which would serve at least a dozen people. Jell-O seemed to be a staple for Sunday supper all over Newfoundland for decades. Inside that Jell-O package was a sweet little bud about the size of a grape amidst the dry ingredients. How often we'd hear Mom bellow from the pantry, "who was into the Jell-O boxes this time?" Of course, this would be several days after we had mischievously sneaked in there (it was usually me, Lock, or Herb) and treated ourselves to that little bud. We knew that we could anticipate her voice yelling a few days after we had helped ourselves, but the temptation was just too great at the time. We were a lot of things, but angelic wasn't one of them.

The three of us would stand around hiding in the pantry, whispering while we handed the soggy bud back and forth among ourselves after a suck or two. We weren't too concerned about hygienic practices at the time. When it had finally dissolved, we would pass those little boxes back and forth, always endeavouring—with some struggle—to make them look perfectly sealed again. But, of course, that never seemed to pan out too well. Poor Mom would always mutter a something about not being able to make dessert without the bud, along with a threat or two, but she was never too angry and always came up with more dessert of some kind. I guess that's why we kept doing it. Unfortunately, we never felt guilty enough to stop digging into her stock, but as they say, boys will be boys.

I remember back in the early days, before our first refrigerator, Mom would send us out with the big bowl of covered liquid Jell-O to place in a bank of snow, hoping it would freeze before Sunday dinner. It all seemed quite normal then, but my grandchildren hear these stories and can't quite believe how we did things back then!

We also regularly visited a building down on Windgap Road, in the Torbay area, which was called Gosse's Wholesale. They were no relation to all the Gosse families in Paradise, though Mr. Paddy Gosse was often asked whether they were. This company fed a flock of people in that area, including us. At the wholesale warehouse, freight from the boats and trains that was a little damaged in loading or off-loading, or that had missed its designated drop-off point, would be sold for quite the discount. And some of these cases of food were next to perfect, but imperfect enough to be discounted. Those little accidents were always good news to us.

Dad walked around the immense stock and quietly assessed some of the discounted cases to ensure that there wasn't too much damage, or that the contents hadn't broken open. Quite often, there would be a sizeable amount of fruit and vegetables that were being sold off. He would divide what he would bring home to the family, and we would help him sell the rest door-to-door as soon as possible, while it remained fresh. There were occasions when we knocked on enough doors to have it all sold before we even got home with our own share. I shake my head, but I miss those days bitterly.

Fresh fruit, at most times, was a rare commodity in Newfoundland, or else it was too expensive for most of us to afford. When people were able to get it cheaply and delivered right to their door, it sold very quickly. I have to admit that I think Dad's mind was always on duty when it came to how and where to make a dollar.

This fruit had been bought and paid for, but even a family the size of ours couldn't possibly eat four or five crates of grapes and bananas before they started to spoil. Grapes were a real delicacy back then, and they were expensive to buy. We would love to see them among the discounts. They were considered a Christmas fruit because most households would break down and buy a few in December to celebrate the season.

Most times, the day after making all these grocery purchases, a few of us would accompany Dad in whatever car or station wagon he had at the time and go down on Topsail Road and around town to sell the quantity of carrots, turnips, grapes, and bananas we had on board. We would all munch on our fill of the fruit along the way, but we still brought home a profit. I cherished those afternoons working alongside my father and a brother or two. It gave us time to talk about how it was when he grew up, what it was like working on all those military bases with the Americans, and all his life experiences, both good and bad, which we found spell-bounding.

Everyone employed at these various wholesale businesses and retail outlets knew Walter Pennell, and they were well aware of all the mouths he was making an effort to feed and support. Of course, Dad or Mom never dealt in anything as small as an actual package of anything; it was always a case. Those suppliers also knew that it was payday for Walter because when he appeared, it was understood that he was on a mission to get as much merchandise as he could for the best price he could. He was a congenial enough man, our father, but after a few pleasantries, he got right to the point. For a man who spoke few words, he struck many a fine deal.

How delighted we'd be when he would point at a crate or box of something we really liked as a gesture to load it up. And load it up we did without delay. All those supplies weighed the back of our car down on the journey home, but when it was all safely stored in our pantry, it truly was a wonderful feeling of full and plenty.

There were large rounds of cheese wrapped in a waxy cheesecloth, which by today's prices would cost over a hundred dollars for one round, barrels of amber pork, fat back pork and beef, huge cloth sacks of flour, and sugar for the bread that Mom produced daily. We would always have cartons of canned Carnation Milk and powdered Carnation milk, large wooden boxes of loose tea, sacks of white navy beans, lima beans, split peas, raisins, yeast, and large bags of puffed wheat, which was always my personal favourite. And, of course, Sunday supper had to include the delicious packages of Jell-O, with or without the bud. If any item was found in a typical Newfoundland pantry of that day, we had it.

Even though I couldn't possibly articulate it way back then, I always admired Dad's consistency and determination even when I was a child and accompanied him to carry the cases out to the car. I could see his eagerness to make our family life as pleasant and plentiful as possible. He was always polite to whoever he dealt with, even if he couldn't strike a bargain. I like to think that I have followed in his footsteps in that way, and I try to get the best for my own family as economically and agreeably as possible. He was so dependable, and for a child, that's a wonderful and warm feeling to be able to count on.

Barter, Share, &
recycle, Paradise-style

Most people in Paradise were an industrious lot who fought for all they could get. Having said that, however, it's true that we also lived among some of the laziest people I've ever had the misfortune to encounter. There were men who never put a workday over them. How some of their offspring survived is a mystery. To be fair to those men, however, a few of the women weren't exactly maternal or domestic either. If you're my age and grew up in Paradise at that time, you would agree with me and probably know exactly the odd creatures I am thinking of. However, wouldn't it be a strange occurrence if all of us were worthwhile individuals? Besides, if there wasn't the odd one, who would we have enjoyed a good gossip about over a cup of hot tea on a weekday afternoon, especially before the wonder of television came to us?

This being said, let's get back to the busy people. Once all the food was eaten and those cloth sacks had been emptied, the women would start the process of washing, bleaching, and hanging them out in the sun to further bleach out any printing that would be on

53

them. Then, what do you think they would do with them? These creative and talented Newfoundland women would dissect them, get out their manual sewing machines, and make dresses and blouses for their daughters, or perhaps a suit for themselves. There was no dress pattern or Google to refer to, nor was there an automatic foot pedal to make it easier. You just pedalled your feet until the stitching was done.

That generation could teach today's society a thing or two about recycling. But to be quite honest, it wasn't done out of caring for our environment as much as it was for stretching what you had to make life more livable. That was always the bottom line.

There was another common (and worthwhile) practice around Paradise Road then. Most residents, of course, grew vegetables in their own gardens. The Pennells did, at times, but if my memory serves me correctly, we mostly grew potatoes. With our family increasing yearly, Mom was far too occupied inside our house changing diapers, washing clothes, or stirring a pot over our woodstove to be weeding outside. And Dad was mostly working out of town on the American bases, and sometimes he was just home on weekends. He didn't have much opportunity to tend to crops.

Growing up, we were often designated assistants to our maternal grandfather, Billy Parsons, on an ongoing basis after school and weekends. We would help with his own new crop of vegetables.

The locals knew that we didn't often grow a vegetable garden, and quite often, they'd come by the house with carrots, turnips, and cabbage, hoping to exchange for some salt meat or pork, which they knew Dad bought by the barrel. So, one of our neighbours would regularly come in the kitchen door, lay down a basket of cabbage, for example, and ask for a piece of meat in exchange. Mom would just nod toward the pantry, as she kneaded her dough or was changing a diaper, and they would go in, find the long, black wrought-iron hook, and pull up a piece of beef or pork out of the brine in the barrel. Then they would hold up and show the size of the piece of meat they had selected as an even swap for the vegetables. Mom would nod her approval, and then they would wrap it in a brown bag or a piece of newspaper, and the transaction was complete.

Depending on who it was, they would more than likely take off their coat and sit in for a cup of tea or a bowl of soup, along with some homemade bread and a chat. Shortly thereafter, off they would go with their fresh meat in tow, and we would have a side order of cabbage included in our supper that night. It worked like a charm for all concerned; we always had fresh vegetables without setting a seed, and those neighbours never ran short of meat. Again, it was that kind of close-knit neighbourhood where bartering was alive and well, and if you could help it at all, you wouldn't see people go without. The whole practice was simplistic, beautifully uncompli-cated, downright wholesome, and best of all, it served us all well.

Amid all the groceries that came through our back door, year in and year out, there was the ever-present barrel of apples available to every child and adult who visited. Those barrels of apples, it turns out, are more of a memory for a good percentage of the population in Paradise than they actually were for the Pennell family. As long as I can remember, there was always a wooden barrel of them placed at the entrance of our back door. They were eaten and enjoyed by most of the children in the community. Their smell would meet you as soon as you entered our house, and to this day, when I smell anything made with apples anywhere, it transports me right back to our back porch.

Quite honestly, there were poor people in Paradise, especially when work wasn't always readily available. I still encounter neigh-bours today who mention with delight the ever-present barrel of apples at the Pennell back door. My father would consistently buy and bring them home, but I have no idea from where. They were replenished so often, not just on his or Mom's grocery trips, that he must have had an agreement with a grocer somewhere close to home. Any child or adult who graced our door was welcome to, and felt comfortable, taking one when they left. It was a given. Let me tell you, it was a genuine case of supply and demand.

Our house was only feet away from the one-room school we all attended, so when recess and lunch time came, with one hop of the fence, there was quite the rush on those apples. During recess, and because we lived in such close proximity to the school, there were often ten to twenty children coming and going in our back porch and kitchen.

Mom would often ask some of the children who their mother or father was, just out of general curiosity, and because as she often said, "They grow so fast, I'm never sure who's who." She always made a point of encouraging certain children to drop in for an apple, and I suspect that she knew that those children were probably hungry for a number of reasons. It could be that the parents weren't working, and it could also be fathers who drank too much of their paycheque.

Florie Pennell never refused anyone's child something to eat, whether it was a meal or an apple, and I personally know a number of those children, now adults that I meet out and about, who still feel indebted to her for this kindness toward them.

I've had people whose families weren't as fortunate as ours tell me that those barrels of apples and Mom's generosity alleviated a lot of their hunger pangs, and the combination went a long way for some residents of old-time Paradise. When one barrel was empty, another one seemed to magically appear. There was never a time when there were no apples. We just took it for granted that they would always be there for the taking. How good did I have it? How thankful I am for it, and for the parents who provided those apples—and everything else!

Out of curiosity, it would be great to actually know how many of those barrels rolled in and out of that house. I would pay good money to lay my hands on one of them now, just for a keepsake. And make no mistake, those barrels were never discarded, because as we have seen, Paradise citizens were the best recyclers long before recycling ever became a fashion.

My paternal grandfather, Jim Rixon for one, would take the barrels apart, stave by stave. From one barrel, anything could be produced: a sled, chairs, or carts. And the metal hoop could be used for rolling, as opposed to hauling cut logs from the woods. Some people would request to have one when it was empty, or as one man used to say, "when she's done!"

I recall asking my grandfather for a nickel one time because my cousin, Roy Parsons, and I wanted to buy ice cream at Gosse's store down on Topsail Road. Now, Grandfather didn't need any wood cut because he always had stacks that he had cut himself, but trying to teach his grandchildren some responsibility, he hesitated and pondered the question. He walked over to the shed and picked up one of those metal hoops that had come off an apple barrel. Then, he instructed us to go get some firewood that he had just cut a short distance in the woods, fill the hoop, and bring it back. Roy and I happily ran in the woods with that hoop to retrieve the wood he referred to. With that task done, we were rewarded with the nickel and contentedly trotted off down to Gosse's Store for the ice cream. It always tasted all the sweeter when we felt we had earned it instead of having it handed over.

We would never refuse Grandfather Rixon anything, money involved or not, because we really loved and respected that old gentleman. It didn't matter that we weren't blood relations.

The Employment
Situation In And Around Paradise, CIRCA 1950

If you were willing to work hard, and most people were, there were various jobs to select from in Paradise. Most of us, at some point in our lives, walked through the doors of several significant companies in the area. Just down over Flint Hill (that steep hill leading up from the main Topsail Road) and less than a kilometre from Octagon Pond, you came to CMIC, which stood for the Canadian Machinery and Industry Construction Ltd. They were manufacturers of industrial machinery.

This five-million-dollar plant was opened in 1952 under the Smallwood Government, and it was a state-of-the-art production and a real boost for the local economy. A plant that was massive and had diverse positions was certainly advantageous and a welcome resource for Paradise residents. A fair majority of the residents in and around Paradise worked as machinists, welders, and general workers. That company was later bought out by McNamara's Industries, which manufactured steel beams, septic and oil tanks as well as asphalt. They also owned a fleet of commercial trucks and operated machinery for constructing and paving roads, and that division was known as McNamara's Construction.

That business was, without a doubt, a vital source of income for many citizens of Paradise, as well as many others all around the Avalon Peninsula. Another real advantage was its convenient location just over the hill in Paradise. You would often hear men who hadn't had any real, steady employment being delighted about being hired at McNamara's. There appeared to be, and quite rightfully so, a sense of stability and pride in having a full-time position that offered decent wages and working conditions. From that decent wage came home improvements, personal advancement, and some degree of flexibility in making purchases.

Along with my brothers, Lock and Herb, I worked there back in the early 1960s when we were seventeen, eighteen, and sixteen, respectively. It was our first 'kick at the can' in the workforce. When we started those jobs, we spent our days lugging, cleaning and whatever else the older fellows didn't want to do—but that was fair enough. We diligently strived to do whatever we were told to do. For the most part, we were everyone's assistants. The bottom line was that we were just delighted to be out of school—and to be that old!

Admittedly, our days of employment there weren't too long; being teenagers with little life experience, we were seeking jobs that were bigger and grander. The three of us moved on to completely different professions, but at the time, we were thrilled to be making a whopping $1.25 an hour, which was good money. When those fat paycheques were in our hands, we kept ten or fifteen dollars for ourselves and were grateful to have the ability to pass over the rest to Mom for our room and board, and to help her and Dad in raising all those other siblings behind us. It was the expectation that when young people started working, they would contribute to the family income. This was mostly done out of respect for their parents. It's a shame that the concepts of "all for one and one for all," and contributing to the family are old-fashioned now. Realistically, however, we really needed to pitch in for the sake of the household's survival. Still, I'm happy to say that the three of us followed that trend. Besides, all we really needed—and thought was important—was some new clothes and money for entertainment on Friday and Saturday nights. How naive we were! But we were enjoying, as the saying goes, "the folly of youth!"

Married men, and some women who managed to get on the payroll at McNamara's, were finally able to progress in life and implement new and improved plans because of their steady work. Families indeed flourished from that weekly cheque, and many individuals reached retirement age working there. The old McNamara building wasn't torn down until 2018, though by that time it was home to Acan Windows.

That site is presently under construction, and it is just about to open its doors once again, with several new businesses opening up in the strip-mall fashion. Obviously, there's truth in the saying that the most recyclable commodity we have on this earth actually *is* the earth, and therefore the sale of land. How unusual it all looks now after passing that plant for sixty years. That building held a goodly store of memories for the local people.

At the beginning of the 1950s, Premier Joseph Smallwood, in his very adventuresome quest to create new industries in Newfoundland, had solicited out-of-province assistance. Enter Alfred Valdmanis, a Latvian who was acting as a consultant to two federal departments and working with Nova Scotia on the establishment of a cement plant. Mr. Valdmanis looked like the proper man for the job that our Joey had in mind.

In 1950 and 1951, Premier Smallwood and several other local politicians visited Germany to inspect plants producing chemical, flour, cement, fish, fish meal, machine, and wood products. Our premier was very impressed with what he witnessed during his visit, and he was quite eager to encourage Mr. Valdmanis to persuade German businessmen to set up shop in our province.

The German people apparently rolled out the red carpet for our premier, known to all of us at home as simply Joey, and his entourage. They were also eager to get an opportunity for advancement after World War II, and here was their chance. Upon the Premier's invitation, they quite readily did set up shop, and thousands of native German families arrived in Newfoundland and worked all over the island. Even though it was only approximately five years since the war was over, with Germany having been our enemy, the workers who arrived were treated very well by Newfoundlanders.

Naturally, some returned to their homeland, but most settled in, learned our language, and many found wives among the locals. Actually, many of these Germans and their families stayed here after their retirement.

There were skilled labourers and technicians in every aspect of the industries that needed to be developed. As a result of Smallwood's association with Valdmanis, German firms established thirteen of the sixteen manufacturing plants created in various parts of the province during the 1950s. There were plants erected for everything from cement, woodwork, tanneries, shoes, gloves, textiles, and even candy, to name a few. And with those plants being erected, employment for locals happily followed. As I'm sure most Newfoundlanders could have predicted at the time, though, some of those ideas were doomed to fail and did.

Among these creations were the aforementioned CMIC and the United Cotton Mills. That building is still standing on James Lane, in St. John's, under another company name. There was also the Newfoundland Hardboards Incorporated and Newfoundland Hardwoods Limited. According to a friend of mine who worked at the Hardwoods plant, they were located close to each other on the railway side of Topsail Road, just east of our first overpass.

Some of those buildings are still standing and operating under another company.

There was also the unfortunate, never-got-off-the-ground Rubber Plant in Holyrood, Conception Bay, which is about a thirty-minute drive from Paradise. The failed Rubber Plant stood vacant for years until it was recently demolished. Also built during this industrious period was a battery manufacturing plant in Topsail, directly across from the Woodstock Restaurant. That building is also still standing.

There was such an immense flurry of activity and significant change in the 1950s when these wonderful new plants and businesses were constructed. I was a boy then when all this first came to be, but I now realize what an incredible shot in the arm all these new establishments were for a significant number of Newfoundlanders. From Paradise and Conception Bay alone, several new plants were opened within an easy walking distance, which was quite an advantage because vehicles were scarce. With these possibilities on our doorsteps, you no longer had to make the laborious trek to St. John's in search of employment, and you weren't forced to till the land or operate a sawmill in order to make a dollar anymore.

There is such a definite comfort in receiving a weekly paycheque and knowing that if you perform your job well and follow the regulations, you will have money coming to you. And that definitely was not, and still isn't, the case in owing your own business or being out there trying to sell your own wares. There is always that element of doubt and that endless feeling of hope that you will be able to pay your bills and support your family when you work privately at any endeavour. There's really no nine-to-five shift when you own your own business. You may be working late hours, as I did in my construction business. However, your mind is always seeking the next project or making a solid effort to complete the task at hand so you can hopefully get paid and move on to the next job.

But gladly, these brand-new companies opening in the Paradise area were sure money, even if the paycheque wasn't always huge. You were steadily employed, and that was a godsend to everyone who worked at these establishments. Most of these new structures were very modern, and they were comfortable to work in. Things were looking up, and people were more content.

According to provincial government statistics, the average hourly wage at these companies in 1952-53, was $0.50 an hour and approximately fifteen to twenty cents less for female employees. Sorry, ladies! It was the norm for the bulk of the twentieth century that males, for the most part, were considered to be the sole breadwinners of each house. However, provincial Government data shows that by 1974, women were progressively receiving the same wage as the men as it was no longer taken for granted that females would or could leave their place of employment to start a family.

With inflation rates rising, females who normally would have wanted to be home rearing the next generation were obligated by escalating costs to produce a paycheque alongside their husbands. It was becoming apparent that two salaries were required to "make a go of it," and that fact has become abundantly clear for today's females and society in general. Many women who were career-minded back in the 1950s welcomed this change, however, and they were eager to have a career and interact in the workplace.

When the Paradise factory doors opened to these employment opportunities, circa 1950, those salaries were quite adequate to provide a sufficient living for the single man in these male-oriented, heavy-duty jobs. But for most individuals who had a wife and family, that payroll cheque had to be stretched to the maximum, especially when there were five or more children to feed and clothe at home.

In Paradise, no one seemed to believe in, or achieve, the two-child standard of today. Maybe it was much colder at night on our hill! The average family included at least eight children, with perhaps an in-law or grandparent thrown in for good measure.

It's worth mentioning that according to an article by Heritage Newfoundland and Labrador, at a time when most Newfoundland people with dependants were merely surviving on a minimum salary, Valdmanis was being paid ten thousand dollars annually by the Smallwood Government. Obviously, there wasn't much need for stretching the dollar there! Most Newfoundlanders were barely making twenty dollars weekly, so an annual salary of $10,000 was inconceivable to most of us.

And it gets worse. According to a 1956 article in Maclean's Magazine entitled "How Valdmanis took Newfoundland to the Cleaners," as Director General of Economic Development (a title he gave himself, by the way), Valdmanis secretly diverted $470,000 of contract money from businesses into his personal account. That immense amount of money went undetected for almost four years. Sadly, the best part of $360,000 was never recovered or restored to the Newfoundland Government. And with a more cynical thought, that's just the sum that was exposed and made known to us! He may have taken much more.

According to that Maclean's article, Smallwood had been so confident in his relationship with Valdmanis that after a perceived extremely successful trip to Germany, where Valdmanis negotiated in the necessary German language, Smallwood increased his annual salary to a whopping $25,000 on their return to Newfoundland. It was later discovered that during that trip, Valdmanis had negotiated for, and was eventually paid, substantial commission fees (kickbacks) by those German businessmen unbeknownst to our premier. It's unfortunate for the Newfoundlanders at home that Joey didn't speak German himself.

Joey Smallwood's right-hand man, Alfred Valdmanis.

Alfred Valdmanis was arrested in April of 1954 for taking kickbacks from the builders of the cement and gypsum plant. The RCMP arrived at Torbay airport here in Newfoundland, and after escorting Valdmanis off a mainland flight, he was detained at our local penitentiary, but transferred to the Newfoundland Hotel pending his trial. How does that work, I wonder? Incarceration at the top hotel on the island isn't exactly suffering, and I guess taxpayers paid the bill there too. This man's charisma appeared to have no limits.

He was eventually sentenced to four years in prison but apparently only served twenty-seven months. After being considered the most influential person next to Joey Smallwood, Valdmanis left Newfoundland for the mainland, pockets full no doubt, and severed all association with our island.

I'm assuming that the levying of higher taxes replaced a portion of that money, but of course, the public was not kept aware of any further financial facts relating to that catastrophe.

Most Newfoundlanders in that period, or even now for that matter, would be incapable of wrapping their heads around a personal bank account of $100,000. I honestly believe that Mr. Valdmanis was quite lucky to have made it out of the province safely before locals became aware of where their tax dollars were going.

However, there was honest work to be had and honest people to do it. And as with all catastrophes, financial or otherwise, we absorb them and move on. Churchill Falls hadn't even been given away to Quebec at this point, and Muskrat Falls would be looming as a nightmare well into the unforeseeable future! But for all intents and purposes, we had jobs, and life in Paradise had significantly improved for us.

The Pennell family shared in these new fortunate opportunities because, as I mentioned earlier, my father was steadily employed by the American Bases. At times, situations arose which enabled him to make a few extra dollars after his shifts were complete.

Building the U.S. Military Base, Fort Pepperrell in St. John's, in the 1940s. Dad worked as a carpenter at that time.

There were other working opportunities on the Topsail Road area. You might catch sight of a panorama of sprawling, new buildings as you came round the bend toward what was commonly known as Donovan's at the time. That wasn't the proper name of the location, but locals referred to that area by that name because of a very well-patronized establishment in that area called Donovan's Hotel. That area now encompasses a busy industrial park, which has actually been named Donovan's Industrial Park.

The first of these buildings was the exceptionally modern plant called Atlantic Hardboard Limited. It was sponsored by the Government of the day and produced residential doors, desks, chairs, office furniture, and a very popular item known as fiberply which was made from pieces of wood glued together under pressure. All these items were in high demand in the 1950s. I've known people from the Paradise area who worked their whole life at the same job and raised a family at these various businesses.

Close to the Atlantic Hardboard Limited, there was a similar plant with different functions. It was the spacious Newfoundland Hardwoods Limited, but to everyone within a twenty-mile radius, it was simply called the Birch Plant. They mostly manufactured plywood, but they had another division manufacturing windows and doors in another building. These divisions worked hand in hand and were all under the umbrella of the Birch Plant. From the 1950s to the 1970s, it was extremely common to see men walking along that section of Topsail Road, with lunch can in hand, on their way to these plants and then home again.

Countless residents from our area became employees of the Birch Plant and never left there to seek other employment. Unfortunately, however, work safety wasn't a priority back then, and many men lost a portion of their hearing through the volume of these machines. Sadly, many men also lost fingers on the machines and saws. It wasn't a daily occurrence for fingers to be severed, but it unfortunately happened to a fair number of victims over the years. It took these awful accidents to finally implement more intense safety measures and safer machinery.

I have a good friend, Gus Connors, now ninety-five years of age, who worked at one of these plants and, very unfortunately, was one of these unlucky employees who lost several fingers on his right hand on a machine known as a veneer clipper. As you can well imagine, it was a horrific experience, and he lost time at work while enduring the discomfort of his injured hand and his new limitations because of the accident.

However, Gus went back to work in another capacity until he retired. He devised a method of handling the wood to maneuver the machinery and did not let his disability hinder him. Not everyone would even consider going near these machines again, but Gus was fiercely determined, dedicated to his work, and actually liked his job. He went on to teach new employees at The Newfoundland Hardwoods Limited how to operate these machines and taught them to have respect for the potential dangers that still faced operators.

All these successful enterprises were instrumental in changing the complexion and importance of Topsail Road. Instead of being regarded as a simple, rural community, Paradise and the surrounding area was now the site of some of the most sophisticated and modern companies, and they were comparable to any province in Canada. It was a real feeling of progress in Paradise, knowing that any man who wanted to be employed actually was.

Not far from these enterprises was the privately owned company of R.W. Barnes, whose workshop and showroom fronted on Octagon Pond. Their specialty was plumbing and heating. That company opened in the early 1950s and offered Paradise residents even more opportunities of employment.

Nearly every single house in Paradise and the surrounding areas, with few exceptions, had an employee or employees of these new companies under their roofs. In my mind's eye, as they say, I can see all those men and women having a chat as they slowly climbed our steep Flint Hill with their lunch cans after their shifts. As I mentioned, I had become one of them for a while in my teens. Through that job, I got to know some of the older men in our community, whom I had only previously known as someone's father. Now we worked and ate together and became familiar with each other as individuals. I believe that further bonded our little community.

In reflection and in all honesty, because Paradise was not a fishing community like most, we were extremely grateful, and downright lucky, to have these establishments within such an easy and convenient distance from our homes in 1952. There was no need to commute, which was a fantastic advantage, and all the people who used to work miles away before now had their job practically on their doorsteps.

In my opinion, Premier Smallwood had great vision in bringing these industries to us. It brought prosperity to an otherwise impoverished island and helped Newfoundlanders put bread on their tables through new work in new industries. It's a calamity that he leaned toward extravagance with Newfoundland's money, that he took his eye off the ball in dealing with so many foreign people, and that he misjudged Valdmanis and others similar to him. And through that misplaced loyalty, significant funds were lost forever.

Now to move on to professions for our ladies! For the females in our community, some employment was available at most of these new companies. However, in the 1950s and certainly prior to that date, the greater population of females who sought employment acquired a position in what was referred to as being "in service." In that case, a girl became a domestic servant in either a private residence or a hotel. This was a time-worn tradition practised all over Newfoundland and Labrador. It was quite commonly known that a young female coming in from around any bay was hoping to go in service.

In many households across the island, and not all well-to-do merchants' residences, either, there would often be a female living in who had come seeking work as a housekeeper, nanny, maid or all of the above. I witnessed many hopeful young ladies arriving dressed in their Sunday best, taking their bags and baggage off the train or taxi into St. John's and surrounding areas, and commencing a career as a domestic worker.

Many young girls and women in Paradise also availed of this opportunity and joined the workforce with the domestic skills they had learned at home. For many of these girls, where they found work they also found romance, often staying and raising a family of their own. I personally know several women who arrived from another part of the province years before, found a job, found a husband, and settled.

Even in my own household during my adolescent years, we had a "girl." That was simply the term we used. A "girl" basically meant an assistant in the home. Our girl just came by day but did not live in. This was undoubtedly because our one-storey house at that time could hardly accommodate the ever-increasing brood Mom and Dad were welcoming into the world, let alone finding space for hired help.

This young lady offered significant assistance to our mother and her youngsters while babies were being born, which was often. This brave young woman would then have maybe six to eight other little Pennells to feed and care for alongside our mother, who was never one to shirk her duties for too long, regardless of the latest childbirth.

I can't recall a point in time, winter or summer, when there was not a line of clean clothes flapping around on our clothesline out in our backyard or wherever there was a free square inch inside the house. The lady Mom had hired always made an effort to retrieve those dried clothes from the back yard, but they would be frozen absolutely stiff in the winter, and you could actually stand up a pair of pants or shirt all on its own. I remember having big overalls standing erect and resembling a headless man. What laughs we would have with that as children! Then they thawed, and the amusement was lost until the next washday. Who needed an iPad to be entertained?

Another advantageous opportunity available to the ladies was securing a position as a waitress or housekeeper at Donovan's Hotel. This establishment was later known as Jerry Byrne's and was located just east of the old overpass on Topsail Road just across the street from the railway tracks.

Originally, there was a railway bed on Topsail Road on the opposite side of the last railroad. It originated behind the site of the Newfoundland Hotel, which was at the extreme end of downtown and ran westerly right across the significant length of Empire Avenue and out of town. You'll often hear older people refer to Empire Avenue as "the old track." It was here that Donovan's Hotel was located, it's doorstep directly in front of the trains.

My mother, during her early youth, was one of the fledgling ladies who was hired on at this hotel and restaurant. It was her first job outside of Paradise that didn't involve working for family, and she was so excited to get started there and earn an actual paycheque.

This lovely two-storey hotel was originally a farmhouse owned by a family by the name of Byrne. In the late 1800s, a widow and mother of three daughters by the name of Keziah Aylward, originally from Petty Harbour, bought the farm, which was in what was then called Western Junction.

Mrs. Aylward initially operated her newly acquired property as a farm with her three daughters and several hired hands for several years. This lady was a real going concern who was known in the area as a fabulous cook and baker. She eventually turned her cooking prowess and managerial skills into a full-time business.

By this time, she had come to know and respect one of her hired workers by the name of Patrick Donovan, whom she regarded as a wonderful and worthwhile man. She went on to marry Mr. Donovan, and together, they built and thrived in their prosperous family business.

Keziah Donovan recognized the potential for growing trade as a restaurateur and inn operator and knew her location would be a likely spot for a stop, if not, the actual first stop on the railroad's way out of town. Her inn was large and comfortable enough to accommodate numerous travellers, and her menu was known far and wide for being second to none.

My grandmother Rixon remembered this place. She spoke of "old Kezzy" Donovan, of people she knew who worked there and how well kept it was. According to Nan Rixon's recollection, Mrs. Donovan was known to be instrumental in the hotel's everyday operation in every aspect. She was regarded as being very devoted to the smooth running of that hotel while being very family oriented. She was what we would refer to today as an entrepreneur in her own right. Mrs. Donovan would even pluck the chickens, ducks, and turkeys that would appear on the menu for that day. Talk about fresh! It must have all been very labour-intensive work, without pre-packaged foods, and certainly no microwaves. I assume that it was all done with just the aid of a woodstove or two and a full staff.

As it turned out, that destination did indeed become the first stop for the train from St. John's, which, of course, added immensely to the hotel's popularity. That first stop was only about twelve kilometres into the journey. For the locals back then, the distance from downtown Water Street to what we was fondly refer to simply as the "overpass" seemed like a substantial outing. Can you imagine? But it was indeed considered a significant distance manoeuvring on dirt road in those horse and cart days, and it was a trek on the train that many citizens made quite happily from St. John's.

In my mother's day, the hotel was still run like a tight ship, with all female workers sporting crisp and clean uniforms. These uniforms, by the way, were purchased by the workers, who were obligated to do that as part of their job description. That was a common practice for numerous trades back then; the thought was that if a worker owned their tools and uniforms, he or she would be more inclined to take care of them and keep them in mint condition. The outfit, worn by my mother and all of her co-workers, was starched and spotless. Stockings had to be perfect, and shoes could never show any signs of wear, but they were polished and shined. She remembers needing nylons before payday and having them supplied to her without charge.

Mom often mentioned her time there when she was just a teenager, circa 1940, and always seemed proud to have worked there. This popular restaurant was adorned with white spotless tablecloths and sparkling floors and windows. Cigarettes were placed, free of charge, in ceramic cigarette cases and laid on each table for patrons' use.

The varied menu boasted of dinners fit for a king, and at the time, all the meat and fish were local and fresh from that week. Mrs. Donovan and her daughters, who apparently succeeded her, insisted on that, and of course, refrigeration was limited, I'm sure. Can you fathom the outlandish price you would have to pay today for a meal of all organic meats, fish, and local, chemical-free produce, along with homemade pies served in an inviting atmosphere with cigarettes free for the taking? It nearly sounds like a high-end Parisian restaurant!

Granted, when it came to the free cigarettes, the horrible things didn't cost thirteen dollars a pack then. Old Mrs. Donovan would turn over in her grave, I'm sure, if she knew how supplemented her income would be for that kind of an exemplary dining experience and service today.

Quite often, people anticipating a weekend getaway or just a sumptuous meal on their longer journey across the island enjoyed the finest service and fare of the day at Donavan's. The train would often drop off a party of residents from St. John's who would just spend the weekend there on a little excursion of rest and relaxation. For some, the treat of getting away from their own kitchen before returning via the Sunday train was most welcome.

Donovan's was known for catering lavish banquets and meetings to many prominent dignitaries, both religious and political.

According to my grandmother, outside of performing your duties, you didn't speak to patrons unless spoken to. A weekend there was certainly considered to be an outing 'in the country' by the populace of that era. Residents of the area were happy to have it as a source of employment and a resource for local farmers to sell their produce.

The Newfie Bullet, true to its reputation as being the slowest mode of transportation on the planet (other than travelling on foot), brought that establishment an enormous amount of trade over the years. Having travelled that train myself many years ago, that's actually not too much of a stretch of the imagination. Passengers would probably have been hungry by the time they finally arrived at the Hotel from St. John's.

Given its reputation for keeping a hospitable and reputable establishment, I'm sure anyone who entered this hotel was on their best behaviour. This was also the case after the business was sold to a Mr. Jerry Byrne, and it continued to be frequented by many people living in the area.

My father often recalled with a chuckle that the young soldiers he transported back and forth from the various bases would be broke when he picked them up on Sunday after spending a great deal of their cheque at the restaurant and bar and enjoying the homelike accommodations offered in the hotel.

Musical entertainment, including accordions, fiddles, and guitars, filled the air with memorable tunes. The locals who lived close to the hotel spent many entertaining nights there, and they met and enjoyed the company of guests from other parts of the world, including these American soldiers.

When Mom was on the payroll there in the late 1930s and early 1940s, there were no unions or maternity leaves. You were punctual, neat, and tidy; you worked hard and you got paid approximately six dollars a week, plus any tips (which usually meant nickels and dimes, but back then, that was significant). You toed the line, showed respect to your employer and their guests, and you kept your job. If you had no transportation to and from work, you had the option of boarding there as well, which Mom did. Being a teenager and working late hours, she happily stayed at the hotel and went home on her two days off. This beat walking home to Paradise in the total darkness.

The operators of Donovan's were known to be strict but fair. Many women started their working lives there and had mostly fond memories of it, as my mother did. It was wholesome and clean, and it was good pay and decent work, especially during the depression.

Some girls met the man who would become their husband there, but I'm guessing that there wasn't much flirting during working hours. One of the perks of that job was that at the end of the day, cigarettes left in the cases on the restaurant tables were yours to take home, as they were replenished daily. Mom would often jokingly say that no one ever had to buy cigarettes in her house because she religiously filled her pockets with the leftovers out of the ceramic cases at closing time and took them home. Otherwise, they would have been thrown out and replaced. That seemed like a perk at the time! In retrospect, the cigarettes should've been left behind.

Moving further east, toward St. John's, there was a really popular restaurant; everyone I know was seemingly employed there at some point in their youth. It was called the Blue Rail, and it was situated on Topsail Road. I'm sure many of you can picture that building as soon as you read the name. For those of you who can't recollect it, it was painted a robin's-egg blue colour for years, and it stood just west of the top of Commonwealth Avenue, coming out of Mt. Pearl. It was a fine old place, and it was owned and operated by a Mr. And Mrs. Fahey.

The Blue Rail Restaurant on Topsail Road (after it was painted white).

The Blue Rail had a cozy interior, with padded booths on a couple of levels, if my memory serves me. You could have a great meal there for a decent price. It was well frequented for years by crowds of people from Mt. Pearl, townies, and residents of my neighbourhood who considered it to be one of their favourite spots. Its doors were open to the public until the late 1970s or early 1980s. A fair number of Paradise adolescents waited on tables or worked in the kitchen out there.

I remember that in our teenage years, my cousin, Roy Parsons, and I walked from Paradise to the Blue Rail for an interview for the lofty position of dishwasher. Mr. Fahey, being the owner, was doing the hiring, and after our so-called interview—for which we were Sunday dressed, I might add—he wanted to hire us both but could only take one. So, he solved the dilemma by asking who was older. We were born the same year but I, unfortunately, was three months younger than Roy. So, Roy was awarded the job. There weren't too many shortlists and employee screenings going on back in the day.

The Blue Rail was a welcoming spot to sit with your friends on the weekend. You could share a hot turkey sandwich or a few drinks and still come out with change from a ten-dollar bill. How sweet it would be to be able to just walk through those doors again, see it all as it used to be, and be twenty-something again! Mr. and Mrs. Fahey never lacked business at the Blue Rail, and it seemed well patronized during all the years it stood there.

There were private enterprises in Paradise as well. The sawmills I mentioned were active daily, with their sound resounding through the neighbourhood. These sawmills catered to all the neighbouring families. Today, it's hard to imagine that people made their own cupboards from scratch, as I did often enough. Actually, it seemed to be quite an extravagance to buy cupboards ready-made at a retailer. It nearly seemed as extravagant as buying a bag of breadcrumbs for making dressing when that first appeared on the shelves in supermarkets and stores. Now, most people buy those ready-made crumbs every day instead of using their stale bread. I think—well, actually, I can say for certain—that my mother and the majority of women of that generation would have thought that to be "the absolute height of laziness," as they all used to say when they were disgusted.

Returning to the sawmills, if you were in the market for a door box or window, Gilbert Lynch and Mose Gosse were the experienced professionals to provide those items. It was a proven fact that Mose Gosse could and did make anything. If you required windows, furniture, or any mechanical job dealing with motors or generators, Mose was your man. He was the epitome of a classic woodworker, and he knew his craft well.

I'm delighted to say that I still see evidence of both of those gentlemen's work to this day. If you happen to see an older house with a wooden window with three one-inch circular air-holes cut into them and a wooden bar to cover them up, you could be looking at the well-crafted handiwork of Gilbert Lynch or Mose Gosse. Just standing around their mills on a summer's day and observing these craftsmen, you could learn quite a deal. I did this, and I applied their know-how to my own construction work.

Both these gentlemen's mills were located at the bottom of Flint Hill on Topsail Road. The shed, which housed Gilbert Lynch's mill, is still standing on Topsail Road. They didn't actually reside in Paradise, exactly, but they were close enough to make a decent living and give excellent service to all of us up over the hill. Their talents were varied because Mr. Gilbert Lynch was a schoolteacher when my mother was a child, and he was always associated with Holy Innocents' School in some capacity or other. His brother, Bert, was married to Mom's sister, Lillian (Parsons).

Mr. Gosse was so well acquainted with our neighbourhood and everyone who lived there that he drove my parents in his beautiful old car to the church on their wedding day. He was the proud owner of a Model T Ford, and it was the only car in the community at that time. It was quite a treat to even have a ride in an automobile back then. Not too many people around can boast of being chauffeured to their wedding in a Model T Ford, but Florie and Walter Pennell could. Mom often spoke proudly of it and how special it felt. I'm assuming that there were no windows made at the mill that day!

Socializing Before
Television

All over this lovely island, for centuries and still to this day, a "game of cards" means 120s (also known as Auction), 45s, or, usually for the men, poker. You may play other card games, but these were by far the most popular ones.

Paradise was certainly no exception when it came to a rousing game of chance. In most of our dwellings during any given week, a group of friends and family would gather at a designated house to play cards.

In Paradise in those days, it was the tradition that only men would attend these games, while the women stayed at home. I'm assuming that women didn't get involved in so-called gambling, as harmless as it was. More truthfully, perhaps, we hadn't reached the age of recognizing that women were allowed a social life outside of weddings and baby showers, and that it would have been the fair thing to do to include them in an innocent game. I believe Paradise was one of the few communities who thought that card-playing was all male.

I can imagine that there would have been a number of perplexed expressions on men's faces back then if someone had suggested including the women in a game of cards. Thankfully, today, many men have stepped up and share in the duties of child-raising. Of course, most women now hold down a nine-to-five job outside the house alongside their partners. All the same, changing diapers, doing laundry, and helping with homework would have been a pretty far-fetched concept for the male population back in the 1940s and 1950s.

Oh, how things have changed, and rightfully so. But back when I was a child, and certainly any time prior, you would never see a man with a baby carriage or staying at home while his wife went out for a game of cards, except in exceptional circumstances. That exception would be the all-female attended bridal or baby Shower, and then women could deal up a storm! It seems peculiar now to have lived in that fashion, and I think we should recognize that family life certainly has progressed in that particular, positive way.

The Pennell home was one of those designated card game spots, with my parents hosting card night maybe twice a week. As per the tradition, Mom never formally joined in the game, but I can see her now, as a couple of us peered out from the bedroom, as she circled the table to see who had the good hand. I don't know if the men minded her doing that, but I'm guessing they wouldn't brook an opinion anyway.

By today's standards, our prizes were, let's say, very economical and practical. But I challenge anyone to say they've ever had more fun, shared more laughter, or that they couldn't utilize the practical prizes given. Everything up for grabs at a game was useful and sought after.

I vividly and fondly recall peering out our front room window with one or two of my siblings early in the evening, in all kinds of inclement weather, and trying to identify the men walking in our lane in the dark. All of them were looking forward to spending some quality time with their neighbours in the warmth and hospitable atmosphere of our kitchen while they sauntered along, clutching their contributions to the night's game.

We also knew quite well, being normal children, that where there was company, there would be a variety of sandwiches and cookies. We were just the kids to make every attempt to gather as much of that as possible without being detected. Of course, most of those evenings were, unfortunately for us, school nights, and we were supposed to be properly asleep before the festivities started. But there was about as much chance of that as us not being eager to relieve the guests of some of that food. I'm absolutely positive that both Mom and Dad knew what we were up to while we waited for their backs to be turned. But there was never anything said unless we got too bold in our attempts and one stern look from Mom was nearly enough to force us to retreat and head back to bed.

All those men would arrive at our house on a frosty winter's night, with maybe a brace of rabbits slung over their shoulder, a partial case of butter, or cans of Carnation milk, shouting their greetings and pleasantries to one and all while shaking off the snow and stamping their feet in the porch. With gaiters thrown in the corner of the porch, each of them, without fail, would quickly make their way to our warm kitchen while spreading their freezing hands over the crackling, hot woodstove. We'd hear them as they happily groaned and muttered their satisfaction with the pleasant feel of the warmth that was reaching them. With a little discussion about how their days were going and a complaint or two about the weather, all hands settled in for a good game of cards.

As children, we would be absolutely thrilled when we caught sight of one of the players arriving happily with their donation to 120s by offering a live hen or two as a prize for the card game. We were certainly used to hens and owned some, but they were never allowed right inside our house except on these nights. Mom had her hands full enough without cleaning up after a hen.

However, if the truth were known, in some Paradise households at the time, hens and other small creatures were allowed in and out! Mom would always make sure they were contained for the duration of the evening until a winner was declared and they were taken off her hands. We would have loved to have taken them in our bedroom for the evening, but the chance of that with Mom on guard was nil!

A humorous incident occurred when a particular man of the community, who didn't faithfully attend, arrived for one of the evening games. Now, this fellow was somewhat of a character—and most might say somewhat of a *shady* character—but he was always pleasant and polite enough. His prize offerings when he did attend generally fell short of most others' contributions. However, on this particular night, as he hurriedly barged through our door, he lifted his arm with a huge smile on his face to display a couple of big, impressive hens! Now one hen as a prize was considered good winnings, but it was extremely unusual for this fellow to offer a hen—and he came with *two*!

Everyone at the table was rather shocked and skeptical as they looked quizzically from one to the other, but they were hopeful of being the winner of these lovely hens. There was uproarious applause at the end of the evening when a winner was declared. We were desperately hoping Dad would win so we could attempt to play with them, but that didn't happen.

There wasn't a word said about the fat little creatures until the very next morning, when Mrs. McCarthy, further down Paradise Road, complained bitterly about having two of her prize hens stolen. Two plus two, of course, pointed directly to our shady character as the culprit, but no one, as far as I know, ever divulged the secret. I'm guessing the person who had won the grand prize certainly didn't speak up. He was never caught, and it was a case of, I believe, "the less said the better." After that card game, he usually presented himself at the house with his usual can of milk or a small bag of potatoes.

This character was a source of amusement to all in the community, and he was always on the lookout for easy gain, which is really a diplomatic way of saying that he would steal the milk out of your tea. I would be remiss if I didn't mention one particular occasion, while he was visiting Donovan's Hotel, which had probably become Jerry Byrne's by then. He secretly confiscated a guitar that had been left by the stage by one of the performers the previous night. On his drunken arrival home, he proceeded to serenade his wife with a rendition of "Alice, Oh Alice." Luckily, her name actually was Alice.

Since he had never played guitar or any other instrument before, his wife decided that she wouldn't put up with the torture of him learning and demanded that he bring it back where he got it. This he did just in time for the following night's performance by the guitar's owner. Whether he was caught or not he never divulged, but he never stole another instrument after that. Well, let's say he never brought another instrument home, but he may have sold one or two on the way. He was an enterprising man but, unfortunately, it was usually with someone else's property.

Back at our house, the prizes for the eventual winner of our biweekly card games were wide and varied. It didn't stop at rabbits, ducks, and hens, as a usual night's biggest win. There would be half cases of butter, pales of salt beef, sacks of flour, potatoes, canned goods, and whatever was left in everyone's pantry that night and might entice the players. No one was out to win their fortune, however, because very seldom did the games go over ten cents.

Most times, pennies and nickels were enthusiastically thrown in the pot, which was placed in the middle of our table. But when dimes came out, you knew the stakes were high, and so was the excited anticipation of what lucky winner would take the pot! All this adult excitement was so riveting to us children. We would listen attentively to every bid and every bit of gossip while taking the opportunity to just generally skylark with each other until we got caught.

Sometimes, if some kind soul caught a glimpse of us peeking into the kitchen, they would sneak a snack to us, unbeknownst to Mom. Although, in reflection, I bet she did know but never mentioned it. Perhaps she wanted us to think that she wasn't aware as she let us have an extra hour of harmless fun while witnessing all the fun the adults were having.

At times, we would push her to the point that she would send Dad in to discipline us. We would hear her say, "Walter, go speak to those children!" Why she bothered, I don't know, because she realized, more than anyone, that sweet, old Dad wouldn't raise a hand or his voice to anyone. He'd open the door of the bedroom, which had been ajar, and just smile and say, "Hello, children! Time to get to sleep now, don't you think?" And that was about as angry as Walter Pennell ever got.

Tablecloths were taken off and put away during these games, and sometimes coins would fall between the cracks in the middle of the table because these chrome sets could always come apart if needed. Remember those sturdy chrome sets with the studded backs and colourful vinyl seats? We always paid close attention in case a coin was dropped in those cracks and disregarded.

The morning after, the very first thing you would do, after rushing to get into your school clothes, was scramble to beat your siblings to the table. We would industriously check all the cracks and the wooden cutlery drawer, which was attached just under the table top. And, of course, the floor under and around the table was always well scrutinized in great hopes of discovering a lost coin or two. Sometimes we got lucky and found a few.

I remember that my brother, Herb, was always the Johnny-on-the-Spot to find and claim the coins first thing. Being the eldest, Herb had more card games under his belt and more experience of where the coins might have fallen. And if it turned out that he retrieved most of the lost loot, he often shared whatever he bought among us. But we weren't fooling around either, so we keenly observed, and we quickly learned from Herb. There was ice cream or comic money at stake, and that's a serious consideration when you're nine or ten.

Oh, those boisterous and joy-filled nights seemed so common-place to us at the time, yet they are so memorable. Looking back, they were as wholesome a bit of fun as could possibly be had. While the men eagerly played, my mother baked bread, washed and pressed children's clothes for the next school morning, peeled vegetables, washed dishes, prepared the "mug-up" for the men post-game, and still saw to one and all's needs.

You hear about people multitasking today like it is a new thing. Florie Pennell juggled various chores simultaneously her whole life and complained about very little, even though she could be a real firecracker when crossed. She was, however, extremely generous of heart, and everyone inside and outside of our house respected her. She was a virtual dynamo and is still fondly remembered by acquain-tances because of it.

Even though Mom didn't play cards with the men, she always encouraged them all to come on in, get warm, find a seat, and make themselves at home. Those card games made the night entertaining for all people concerned, even if you weren't playing.

Lying in our beds with no intention of sleeping, we could hear the friendly bickering, the pounding on the kitchen table when someone presented a good card, the continuous bluffing, the uproar of laughter, and the enthusiastic patting on the back of the winner when one was declared. And what a sweet, sweet memory it is!

The proud winner became the new owner of a brace of rabbits or a small pale of riblets to contribute to his family's Sunday dinner. And the person who supplied the grand prize got the pile of coins in the middle of the table. It always seemed like a win-win situation to me. It was the best game of cards around and no one took it too seriously. I always longed to be old enough to join in, get a chance to win the big prize, and show all those adults what a good card player

I was (even though I wasn't). But you know, it wasn't the card game I loved, but rather the camaraderie I witnessed.

Once the winners enthusiastically gathered up their prizes, the cards were carefully put away for the next card night. The kitchen table was quickly cleared, and my mother, who had busily circled the table periodically like a mother hen, laid out the post-game spread. She was a provider to the utmost degree. Not a living soul ever stepped out over our doorstep hungry, whether there was a card game or not.

The big kettle, with years of burnt-on soot on and around the bottom was full of boiling water. It would have steamed on the stove all evening, and by evening's end, it would finally be put to use. A teapot with loose tea leaves was filled to the brim. As a matter of fact, I can never remember that kettle *not* boiling for family and friends. It was always ready for the next visitor to our house. I doubt it ever went cold on our stove.

Next, all players were invited to a hot, steaming cup of tea and an ample supply of raisin buns, homemade bread, jams, preserves, and whatever your heart desired before you donned your coat and gaiters and ventured out into the cold night air.

By this time, my siblings and I would finally be in bed, but we were never asleep on card night. I'm sure Mom must have accounted for our participation earlier in the day while deciding the amount of tea buns and cookies she would need for the game. It was a waste of time for her to bake less than a couple of dozen of anything in our house anyway, company or not.

I'm totally grateful, at my age, to have experienced all those wonderful evenings in my warm, cozy, little abode just off the main road. As little children, we stored all the laughter, joking, and neighbours appreciating neighbours in our minds, not having any idea that we'd be looking back on it all so fondly.

There were homes in Paradise at that time that didn't have what we had. They didn't have the food, for one thing. That was a common dilemma in the early days, and I remember children in school being genuinely hungry. Some of them, I'm sorry to say, didn't have the care and protection of two good parents, which they certainly deserved.

And as I reminisce and nostalgically smile to myself, I can honestly shed a tear or two remembering the satisfaction, joy, and unmistakable friendships that those nights brought to all in the tiny village.

I can still hear our company leaving, still enthusiastically discussing and laughing about the game, the back door closing with everyone declaring, "Thanks and Goodnight," and the sound of all their voices trailing off outside while they walked down our lane. Then you'd always hear Dad banking down the woodstove for the cold night, Mom busying herself getting the table ready for the morning, and then finally there'd be silence.

It was the end of another successful card night in the Pennell home, and there was probably another confused neighbour the next morning scratching their head while counting his or her hens.

Holy Innocents':
Paradise's Multi-Purpose, One-Room Schoolhouse

In the early 1950s and onward, all my siblings and most youngsters in the area attended a typical rural one-room schoolhouse with, you guessed it, a big, black, hopping-hot woodstove right in the middle of it. That lovely stove was given to a former student, Wallace Lynch many years later. I visited Wallace's home one day, and I was delighted when he showed me his woodstove and stated that it was the same one from our old schoolhouse. I'm also delighted to state that it's still operating to its full potential under Wallace's care.

How long ago it all was! But I can distinctly remember arriving for my first day of school and sitting in a long, three-seater desk, the ones with the old inkwells in them. Dressed to the nines at the tender age of six, I shared that lovely old antique desk with Jackie and Rosalie Lynch, who were every bit as scared as I was.

Once they managed to graduate to a certain grade and were a little bigger and heartier, it was expected that students, in their turn, would come to school a little early with a bag of splits and a couple of junks of wood in tow to light the fire and get the school defrosted. It was your responsibility, even if you were only ten years old. Can you imagine that responsibility, involving *fire* no less, given to a mere child these days?

There weren't any thermostats to ensure that the classroom would be warm enough for the comfort of its pupils. On most days, especially during the winter, when the heat had finally circulated around our small school and it was very comfortable in your desk, it was nearly time to pack up and go home.

Can we fathom our grandchildren today having to endure the cold for at least half the school day because the School Board provided inadequate heating? It wouldn't be tolerated. But back then it was, at least in our neck of the woods. I'm thinking, perhaps cynically, that being a small area with a small population, we weren't regarded highly enough by the powers that be who sat on the School Board. I feel justified in making that statement because it was a known fact that schools in St. John's were heated back in the early 1940s.

It's sad to say that it wasn't until nearly 1960 that our reliable old woodstove was replaced with modern heaters for the comfort of the students and the teachers. It was terribly negligent that so many small children were so cold for so many years when it could have been prevented.

As the Pennell house was so close to Holy Innocents' schoolhouse, and I mean literally feet away, and because so many of us were students there, it was very often our first job in the morning to gather up some kindling and paper, some coal, and a junk or two of wood. The students, and therefore their family, provided the heat for the school.

I remember scratching the frost off the bedroom window on wintry mornings and peering out to appraise the day when you would first woke up. Of course, that was after you had the courage to leave your snuggly and toasty bed, which you shared with your brothers, and got your clothes on at Olympian speed. Next, we'd venture out into the frosty morning, even before we had a bite of breakfast, and hop the fence between our property and the schoolhouse with an armful of wood and all the fixings. You would rush into the schoolhouse, throw the load you carried down at the foot of the old stove, open its door, and commence lighting the fire as quickly as was humanly possible.

The old reliable woodstove as we had at Holy Innocents' Schoolhouse.

I recall, like it was yesterday, that the door to the schoolhouse was always open. You certainly didn't waste any time because it was so absolutely frigid in there. You'd see your breath with every puff as you worked diligently to get the job done. You'd light the match to the kindling or a bit of paper and pray that it caught as soon as possible. Meanwhile, you rubbed your hands together, jumping up and down in an effort to get your blood circulating. When it did finally ignite, you'd let out some expression of glee—at least I did—at the most welcome flame. When you were satisfied that it would stay lit, that the room would be a step up from freezing at 9:00 a.m., and that you could hear the wonderful crackle of the fire with the stove door shut, your chore was complete. Then, in a flash, you'd hop that fence again and run as fast as your two feet could carry you to your own warm kitchen and some hot porridge or homemade toast.

I'm sure some of my readers who attended Holy Innocents' School can well remember taking their turn during those harsh, freezing winter days. We all begrudgingly took our turns so the heat could be somewhat generated by the time students arrived. It was a poor set-up, though, and it certainly wasn't adequate or conducive for learning.

It was a common occurrence then that whatever child had the morning chore of lighting the stove would very quickly jump the fence once their task was done and sit in with our family for breakfast and something hot to drink. We all knew each other, and there was a Pennell in nearly every grade. I don't know if the School Board expected those children to walk back to their own home after lighting the stove, or if they were just complacent enough to expect them to stay there, freezing until school started. Regardless, those students quite often found their way over to the comfort of our kitchen, had a bite to eat, and left for school with us.

At the Pennell house, no child was ever turned away, no matter what the temperature happened to be that day. I wouldn't hazard a guess of how many days there would be someone extra at our meals, both morning and night, either child or adult. It was never questioned. To be honest, there were so many of us that I don't think Mom could keep track of who was whose friend regardless. And as long as you behaved, you stayed. It was just normal for us to have company, and that dynamic was always the same.

This fire-starting chore, by the way, was a non-paying job, of course, and all pupils were expected to contribute to the wood supplies for the day. Everyone who was old enough, and that meant if you were out of Grade Two, was expected to take their turn. There weren't too many child labour laws in effect back in the day. But even if there had been, for me personally, I felt the responsibility to make sure my younger sisters and brothers weren't too cold when they arrived. At least we were allowed to keep our coats on if it was unbearable, and that was usually all winter.

It was, of course, a substandard building for the time, but we used to like to think that it was more modern than that because there was a long, folding door that separated the various grades. We then had "two rooms" in our schoolhouse, which seemed pretty sophisticated to us. Finally graduating to the upper grades, which were on the other side of that door, was a feeling of accomplishment in itself.

It was the female students' job to scrub the floors of the school and clean the windows and blackboards every couple of weeks, usually on the weekends! It's nearly laughable now to think that students, some of whom were quite young, were expected to come back to school on their supposedly free weekends, unsupervised, to perform housekeeping and sometimes a little maintenance. But that's exactly how it was, and it was just accepted.

I'll share a memory with you now, and not too pleasant a one. It has always struck me how poorly the incident was handled.

On one particular weekend, Eli Rixon, Harvey Janes, cousins Tex Janes and Roy Parsons, and I went into the schoolhouse because we noticed the girls hadn't come down to clean for some reason. Obviously, with nothing better to do (because I'm pretty confident it wasn't our school pride), we cleaned the school from top to bottom and left it shining like a new penny. That Monday morning, the teacher, Mrs. Ingram, remarked how sparkling the school was and congratulated the girls on a job well done. Ivy Lynch spoke up and told her they hadn't done it, but the boys filled in and completed their tasks for them. Well, instead of commending us on our hard work and initiative, Mrs. Ingram was stunned and became infuriated, wanting to know what boys had come in the school. I'm sure she was aware the school was left open day and night, month in and month out, and we weren't trespassers.

Well, for those of you who remember those times, you could always rely on Tommy, whose last name won't be mentioned, to tell the teacher all the names as quickly as he could blurt them out. Poor Tom, I don't think he meant to be a tattletale, but he never missed an opportunity to supply information. With that, she angrily called—or I should say shouted at—us to come to the front and proceeded to strap each of us several times. I don't think Mrs. Ingram understood the principle of positive reinforcement. It was more of a "spare the rod and spoil the child" kind of mentality with her. Our good deed earned us a pair of sore hands and an unhealthy dose of humiliation. What was the woman thinking?

Isn't it curious that we were always allowed, and strongly encouraged, to enter the school with our own supplies to light the fire for the stove in the mornings? By the way, neither Mrs. Ingram, nor any of the teachers who taught there for that matter, ever came in early to do that uncomfortable job. Suffice it to say that none of the boys ever took it upon themselves to use part of their weekend to clean the school again either!

Another not-so-attractive venture was the emptying of the toilets. Yes, you read it right. That was also part of our non-negotiated "job description," even though we didn't have a paying job. I, as well as many others, started the school day frozen to death trying to light the fire and ended the school day trying to successfully empty toilets after a day's use. Academics always seemed easy compared to those duties.

Why the school board never employed a maintenance man or woman for our school is mind-boggling. After all, it was the 1950s, not the 1850s! But every afternoon, rain, shine, or snowstorm, the boys (usually) would have the despicable chore of emptying the toilets. There was limited plumbing in our school, so out we would go with our buckets at 3:00 p.m., directly across the road to the bog pit. Making every effort to keep our feet dry, we would scoop up pail

93

after pail of bog water, struggle back to the school with the heavy buckets, and manually flush the toilets.

I can remember my cousins, Tex Janes and Roy Parsons, and me muttering under our breath while we trudged along the road with those heavy pales. One day, Tommy (the same Tommy who shall remain nameless) hooked my cap off my head right directly into the toilet, never to be seen again. Of course, what would you do with it even if you *had* found it? Since it was knit by Mom, as all our hats and mitts were, I felt obligated to tell her what had happened to it. I was tickled to death that I didn't have to go back to retrieve it!

It's absolutely incomprehensible these days to think that at the end of every school day, a ten- or twelve-year-old-child was expected to carry out a disgusting chore such as that. It wouldn't happen now, and in fairness to all of us who endured it, it shouldn't have happened then. There wasn't even the chance of getting into a little harmless mischief with that job. Mischief, yes, but not harmless! However, we managed, as most boys do, to find a little mischief elsewhere.

Our school was divided into two areas by that wonderful folding door, with Grades One to Four on one side and Grades Five to Eight on the other. All one grade was in a particular row. With each grade you passed, you moved one row closer to the window. That window seemed awfully far away when you were in Grades or Rows Three and Four. But each year, we inched our way toward that window, and eventually out the door, with no more fires to be lit or toilets to deal with.

Teachers at Holy Innocents' in the 1950s, L-R: Miss Bragg, Mrs. Power, unidentified.

However, on the brighter and happier side, on certain nights, our versatile school became a Broadway stage or a Cinema for all Paradise residents who were interested in attending whatever play or movie was being featured. There would be no announcements or flyers going around. It was all word of mouth, and everyone was kept in the loop of the entertainment that was up-and-coming.

One of my favourite memories was a school play called *The Old Man and the Old Woman*. The whole play took place in a cardboard cut-out of a dory, which we all contributed to and coloured. It was christened "Lukey's Boat," just like the Newfoundland song, and that was painted on the outside.

My sister, Florie, was the old woman, and my cousin, Tex Janes, was the old man. I remember Mr. Smith, our teacher, playing the organ to the tune of "Lukey's Boat." There we were sitting on little stools behind the cardboard cut-out wearing our oil skins and sou'westers, pretending to be seasoned fishermen while rowing our makeshift oars. I felt like a movie star.

There were a few lines of dialogue to the play, but we forgot them, stole each other's lines, fooled up the whole skit, and ended up trying to row the boat while in a fit of laughter—as was the audience. We ended it—and were thankful that it was over—by singing "The Squid Jiggin' Ground." We received thunderous applause and were told how hilarious it all was. To this day, people still think it was supposed to be a comedy skit, and I still agree with them! Anyway, it was far better our way.

On many of these social evenings, cousin Tex Janes, "the Old Man" from the Play, and I would be more than willing to get there early to get the old pot-belly stove pumping out the heat for the anticipated audience. You didn't mind as much then because school-work didn't follow lighting the stove, and often it was still warm from the school day. Tex and I would work at the canteen during the night, and our paycheque was a bar and a bottle of "beer," but at times we ate more than we sold.

Pop wasn't called pop or soda; it was simply referred to as "beer," and when children asked for a bottle of beer, it was naturally assumed they didn't mean Blue Star or Dominion. They meant cream soda, coke, or birchy beer as we called it. Remember those? I'm sure many of you can make that happy trip down memory lane to a day when we were that innocent and carefree.

Every few months, there would be rehearsals for a new play, which would be taken very seriously by the children and delivered with the greatest effort their talent could offer. These plays were performed on special occasions through the year (usually at Christmas, Easter and the end of a school term or school year). It was as exciting to us then to be involved in the concerts as if we were performing on the stage of the Arts and Culture Centre. All the desks would be pushed back, and approximately one hundred chairs, which was the maximum capacity allowed, would be set up in rows in anticipation of the big audience we were bound to draw.

On other occasions, eight-millimetre movies and a projector appeared, and all of Paradise would come out to see the "new release," even if it was a few years old. A canteen with drinks, chips, candy, and other goodies was sold to the audience—by the children, no less—and it was as much fun, if not more, as any professional cinema. We might not have offered cheese-covered nachos or those large vats of popcorn they have today, but the items in our canteen didn't cost a significant portion of your day's pay, either.

When there was an upcoming wedding or a new baby on the way in Paradise, the school was used for all the wedding showers and baby showers in the area. All the women in the community would industriously work on gifts for both kinds of occasions, knitting and crocheting weeks, and sometimes months, beforehand.

All my sisters, many of whom had their wedding and baby showers at Holy Innocents'. Bottom, L-R: Janet, Michelle, and Brenda; Top, L.-R: Jane, Florie, Joan, Lilly, and Ruby (Doreen is missing)

Me and Mom have a waltz at a "Time."

There was a kitchen in the school, where, most importantly, a kettle could be boiled for tea, which was the main component of any decent shower. It was definitely expected that if you attended one of these showers, you brought along a plate of food to contribute toward it. I can remember staring with wonder at the numerous plates of sandwiches and a wide variety of cookies. As Mom attended each and every one of these events, because she knew everyone, we often would wait anxiously for her to come through the door home. We always knew that she would have a plateful of whatever was left over.

Aunt Marg (Parsons) Hussey, Mom's sister, with Mom on the right

It was a common practice for all women at showers, in Paradise and neighbouring communities, to divide up and take home whatever was left. You left home with a plate of food and you came home with a plate of different foods. We always thought it was a wonderful concept, especially when there were all these different kinds of cookies from those our own mother made. As boys, we would be delighted to hear of an upcoming wedding or a baby on the way. Even though it was a waiting game for us, as well as the bride or mother-to-be, we knew that eventually, the day would arrive and we could happily anticipate a feast of some sort.

From these showers, the mother-to-be went home with a bounty of new clothes for the new arrival, and the bride-to-be had every kitchen gadget and cuptowel she could carry. There was no special theme, no decorations, no store-bought cakes, or anything too fancy or expensive. But all the women in Paradise thoroughly enjoyed an invitation to sit down and rest for a while in the now-warm schoolhouse as they caught up on the latest news, and, of course, gossip with their neighbours. It was their answer to Tim Horton's: they could relax in each other's company and have some fun for themselves at the end of a laborious day.

The schoolhouse also passed as a venue for the biweekly card games. People came from practically every house in Paradise, and even from St. Philips, a distance away to share in a good game of 120s. This was organized in an effort to make some money for our Church. These card games involved both men and women, as opposed to private card games, which only men played. All players arrived with their own "cards and baskets." The baskets were, of course, full of food for the after-game lunch.

Children enrolled in Holy Innocents' were informed of the upcoming card game and were asked to have their parents contribute food from their family pantry as a donation. When the donations were brought in, first, second, and third prizes were arranged.

The lucky winner of the first prize went home with a full and bountiful food hamper. The second prize would be perhaps a bag of flour, a bag of sugar, and a couple of cans of good old Carnation Milk. The third, of course, would be a smaller sample of the same, with maybe a bag of split peas thrown in. There was always a small door prize as well, with something like a pound of butter, a jar of homemade preserves, and a couple of loaves of homemade bread. It all depended, of course, on what was brought in as donations. These games were always well attended, especially when you had the chance of bringing home groceries.

There were so many of us Pennells enrolled in our school that after each of us contributed a tin of this and a bag of that toward the hampers, we would consider ourselves to be quite lucky if Mom won back just a portion of the donations.

Those were certainly lovely times! But not all of my memories in that schoolhouse were pleasant or humorous. We had a horrific incident at one point which changed two teachers' lives forever. I witnessed one of the biggest fusses that ever happened within its walls, and it involved my own mother and sister.

A new male teacher was helping himself to the groceries, which the students were bringing in to be stored for the night of the card game. The parents knew what they had contributed via their child or children, and after several card games, the locals became quite aware of their missing offerings. After prizes were distributed, residents made a point of looking to see if his or her donation had made it to the prize boxes. A fair amount of the food and other donations that had been left in this gentleman's care were definitely on the missing list, and the locals were not happy about it either. People were speculating, but all fingers were pointing to him as the culprit. And if that wasn't bad enough, it actually got worse for that teacher.

At the very same time that neighbours were upset over the loss of the prizes and wondering how to approach this teacher, one of my younger sisters, who was only about ten years old at the time, came home late for lunch from school, just as we boys were leaving to return. When she and my sister were alone, my mother asked her if she was sick, as she looked upset, and then my sister meekly dropped a bombshell.

As Mom recalled years later, my sister didn't know what this male teacher's intentions were, but our mother certainly did when she was made aware of the details! This man kept my little sister from going home to lunch and then proceeded to make advances toward her. How frightening and confusing that must have been for her.

Now anyone who knew our mother at all also knew that when provoked or had her children interfered with, her temper was a match for the devil himself. And she was having none of it. It was a situation which called for zero tolerance, and that's precisely what she had.

As I had earned my way academically each school year and was getting closer to the window by this time, I literally had a front row seat to the unfolding drama that took place. I can quite vividly recall spotting Mom just as school reconvened for the afternoon. She was storming down the lane toward the school, hurriedly pulling dough from her fingers and flicking it on the road with a vengeance, as she had been in the middle of a batch when my sister came home. Her skirts and apron were flying and the dust from the road was visible as she picked up speed, and I'm sure her nostrils must have been flaring.

I felt nearly dumbstruck as I watched her stomp down the road, trying to recall what I had been up to in the last few days. I thought that she might have discovered one of my shenanigans and was now coming to get me. But upon quickly rewinding the events of the last several days in my head, I was coming up innocent. The teacher had also noticed the individual rapidly approaching and looked intently out the window. He obviously wasn't too familiar with our mother, because if he had been, any ill intentions he might have had toward my sister wouldn't have occurred.

Upon seeing that it was Mrs. Pennell, and that she was making a rapid beeline toward the school and obviously picking up on her demeanour, he took off like a scald cat into our cloakroom, which he had selfishly changed into an office for himself. He slammed and locked the door with such a force that all the students bolted upright, looking around confused, knowing that there was something definitely wrong.

Mom didn't knock on the door but barged right in with an entrance that would have put Arnold Schwarzenegger to shame. I was petrified myself as I watched in horror, wondering what in the world was wrong with my poor mother. I would have known had I been made aware of the horrific details she had learned from my sister.

She loudly asked where the teacher was and we all nodded, in quiet astonishment, at the cloakroom. Without missing a beat, she then proceeded to pound with both fists on that cloakroom door and demanded, at the top of her voice, that the "bloody coward" come out.

This unbelievable scene with my mother continuously banging on the cloakroom door went on for a minute or two. Next, the female teacher, who had been in the other area behind the folding doors, came in and furiously questioned Mom about what she was doing. When this teacher came to the realization that acting authoritative was not having the desired effect on Mom, she tried to appease her. She unfortunately didn't know that there was no intimidating our mother, and appeasing her wasn't going to work either.

The lady calmly asked for an explanation for Mom's behaviour, so she promptly gave her one. The reasons that Mom gave her, which I can remember being short but certainly not sugar-coated, were probably not shocking news for this teacher. She happened to be the unfortunate wife of the coward who was still hiding and probably shaking in his boots in his makeshift office. No one liked this teacher anyway, but I remember feeling afraid for the poor creature had that door opened.

Eventually, Mom gave up on trying to fiercely yank that door open to confront him and reluctantly went home with a loud warning that "You can tell him that this is not over yet!" And with that declaration, she left as quickly as she had entered. He didn't realize what a volatile pot he had stirred.

I watched my house, which was just next door. Barely a few minutes passed before she came out in her coat and hat, with handbag swinging by her side. Our mother was losing no time as she walked out Paradise Road at breakneck speed, heading toward Flint Hill. I recall staring at her until she was out of sight. I guess I was concerned for her because it definitely wasn't a daily occurrence for her to be that upset, and I recall having the odd thought of the obvious severity of the event if she was leaving the bread she was making unattended. Like everyone else in the school, we were totally perplexed as to what was going to happen.

I definitely knew one thing, and that was that I was really relieved I was not in that teacher's shoes. He timidly poked his head out of the cloakroom door in the hopes she was gone. He may have hidden temporarily, but he didn't have a snowball's chance in hell of escaping Mom's wrath now.

On that walk, she went directly to one of the School Board officials, who lived close by on Topsail Road, and told them her story. And when Mom was mad, diplomacy went straight out the window; she told it just as she saw it.

When we arrived in school the next morning, we were anxious to see how Mr. Smith was faring. The surprise was on us, however, because we had no teacher at all! Mr. and Mrs. Smith were sent packing, as the expression goes, and if the truth were known, none of us missed either one of them. They were both contrary individuals, and they made for a long school day. I believe it took another day or so before a replacement came.

As school days went, that was probably the most entertaining afternoon any of us had ever had at school. Unsurprisingly, Mr.

Smith immediately cancelled the rest of the school day after the fuss. Mom was pretty popular for closing the school for a few days until our new teacher was welcomed to Holy Innocents'.

After that fiasco, no food items were ever missing from the Card Night hampers either. Oh, to have been a fly on the wall in the house of that husband-and-wife teacher duo that evening. It's perhaps fortunate for all concerned that our mother didn't have his home address. Our lives returned to normal after a week or so, but I doubt very much that his did!

Every Sunday, the school was turned into an Anglican Church. The curtains were opened on the stage, and the mobile pulpit put in place up on the stage. The desks were taken out, and the chairs remained but were turned around to face the stage instead of the blackboard.

There was also an old organ there for years, and if you were talented enough and could beat out a hymn or two, you were the official organist! That was the only criterion for that job. We had a couple of local people who played for the Sunday service, and that little schoolhouse took on quite a religious air as we reverently regaled the neighbourhood with those hymns.

There was a church bell and tower as well, and you would hear that bell peel every Sunday for the 10:30 service. The rope for the bell was tied up at a height that the young boys couldn't reach and play with, even if you piggy-backed relentlessly! Of course, as young boys, we wouldn't have dreamt of anything that mischievous.

Mr. Ches Lynch, who lived on Topsail Road not far from our road was a warden with the School Board. And it was Mr. Lynch's job to ring that bell for Church to bring all Paradise parishioners out on a good and holy Sunday. It was also his job to ensure that all students attended school regularly, and he was strict about it. If you were inclined to take a day off without your parents knowing about it, he somehow always got wind of it. And if you did get caught, you had to face him and our parents. Those odds were not too enticing.

In hindsight, though, if he hadn't been strict, we wouldn't have gotten half the education we did.

The little old Holy Innocents' schoolhouse was, without a doubt, the most well-utilized building around. It served us well (once it warmed up in the mornings) as a school, a church, a venue for baby and bridal showers and card games, a cinema, a theatre, and a place for all residents to meet and enjoy an evening out. Periodically, there would be dances for the adults in the area, and being so close to the school, we would often be able to hear the violins and accordions late into the evening. You would also hear all the men outside getting a breath of air while having a chat and perhaps sneaking a "whet" or two. A whet was what all the old-timers called an alcoholic drink.

On warmer days in the summer, the old schoolhouse hosted garden parties, both inside and outside. My brothers, friends, and I would get the opportunity to admire all the young girls from the neighbouring St. Philips and surrounding areas. There were a few romances initiated in that little building, which, of course, led to wedding showers, baby showers, and so on. The sandwich trays were never put away for long.

We were so close to the school that functions sometimes spilled over into our garden. If the weather was hospitable, people lingered for hours. They were really pleasant events, especially for hungry boys, if my memory serves me.

Holy Innocents' wasn't a big or well-constructed structure, and certainly not a fancy one, but it served our community extremely well at the time. It was the focal point for all the community. We used it faithfully and were glad to have it. If only it had had electric heat, it would have been perfect!

Homemade Stills &
Outwitting The Law

I don't imagine that it comes as any shock to readers who are about my age to know that there were numerous operational "stills" in Paradise in my time. Actually, they were operational but well hidden long before that. The necessity for the still was felt keenly all over the island because liquor outlets were a scarce item then. If you lived in one of the bays and liked the odd drink, you either had to have connections to buy legal alcohol, which would have been a fair distance away, or you simply and illegally made your own. It was quite a common practice for families to have "on a brew," and even though it was illegal, it was quite calmly and readily accepted.

These stills were, of course, like the product they produced: homemade. They came in a variety of types and were manufactured following time-worn patterns and plans, passed down over the years from generation to generation. I don't think hygienic concerns were uppermost then, but a germ wouldn't have a chance anyway against the hundred percent or more proof moonshine being produced. But no matter the quality or type of still, they all had the same result: liquor of some sort.

Stills were placed so that they would never be obvious to the naked eye. I think it would be pretty accurate to say that it was also understood by the powers-that-be that a fair majority of houses in Paradise had some sort of homemade still or contraption that would pass for a still on the property. It was widely known that the authorities kindly ignored these stills, maybe knowing that they would be the recipients of a few bottles later on. The residents were also a little discreet for the most part, depending on who was looking.

I can never honestly remember seeing any sort of liquor paraphernalia lying around a property, but you would actually discover a fully operational still at times in or out of people's houses. Oftentimes, these stills were well disguised. Many people actually had them in a back room of their kitchen, which served many domestic purposes. Placed in with the various domestic tools, plus the various buckets and pails (including the 'night soil' pail), it was felt that if you received a visit for any reason from a government man, they wouldn't be inclined to snoop around in there too quickly.

How no one was ever actually poisoned or went officially blind from this homemade stuff is a mystery. It was more potent and powerful than any of the current distilled and government-issued liquor. To say that it would put hair on your chest is an understatement. Some of the old-timers could make "a drop of stuff" that would bring a tear to your eye. And on top of that, most of them drank it straight, as they carefully scooped it up with a dipper out of the pale.

Up to the 1950s, soda pop was not a popular item in most houses. When someone had an alcoholic drink, it would be mixed with water or, as I said, served straight up. It was not totally unheard of when the fermentation time arrived, and the men proceeded to draw off a batch and sample their newest bottle, to the find the odd, happy man a few hours later lying in a ditch singing to the top of his lungs. He had, of course, failed miserably at trying to wend his way home. These poor fellows were rendered senseless and legless, I might add, once they got into some moonshine and had to be escorted home by some kind soul passing along.

I recall one night it was my turn to help a neighbour out of a ditch as my mother looked curiously out our kitchen window and witnessed him staggering slowly down the road. She despised seeing men drunk, yet she was concerned for their welfare because they were all neighbours. "Ches," she called, "put on your coat and go out and make sure poor old Mr. So-and-So keeps to the road." In the few minutes it took for me to get into my jacket, out our lane, and walked down the road a few feet, there he was—horizontal but happily lying on his back down in the ditch. I laughed when I heard him singing his rendition of "Roses are Blooming, Come Back to me Darling." Well, what a state the poor creature was in, between the mud on the outside and the moonshine on the inside. But with my assistance, he made it home to an equally disgusted wife, who muttered to herself as she carefully put him to bed. That often happened when a brew was finally ready for consumption. The old-timers may have thought it was ready, but I don't think they realized how lethal it really was, and maybe should not have consumed as much. However, watering down wasn't a common practice.

There could have been amputations performed on some of these individuals' limbs when they got into a homemade batch. They undoubtedly wouldn't have felt a thing. According to my father, you always knew the few men in the neighbourhood that would happen to, and the locals religiously kept a friendly eye out for them on their homeward journey. Oh, how the poor wives endured those nights! I'm sure that none of them were ever too surprised.

There was, however, never a still of any kind in our house, simply because Dad was never a drinker. I don't know if he ever took even a social drink; he would offer it to company in our house when he had it at Christmas or some special occasion. Mom would have the occasional drink and kept some in the cupboard for medicinal purposes.

She would have some in a hot water bottle for some reason, for when a female neighbour would drop by because her husband was under the weather. Being 'under the weather' seemed to be code for hung over back then and out would come Mom's hot water bottle. Depending on the degree of the "sickness," she would ration it out in a cup for the woman. Sometimes, she would pass over the entirety of the contents of the hot water bottle. It was always duly returned to her empty with the unspoken understanding, I'm guessing, that it would be partially full when sickness struck again.

Along with those party nights, the men would break out their pipes or a plug of tobacco to make the drink totally enjoyable. In our house, cigarettes were held in high esteem. Those were the things that Dad adored, and he was never without them. Cigarettes were never as popular as they were during the war years, and it seemed that once you reached a certain age, you just automatically took up the habit.

Did we ever imagine the day would arrive when a package of those awful things would cost close to fifteen dollars? The Americans from the various bases gave them away for pastime, and the price of them was nowhere even near a dollar at that time. Lucky Strike, Chesterfields, and Camels, in their unfiltered form, all wrapped in their soft packages, could be found in any household. I would say that most children back then grew up in a blue fog from all the clouds of smoke in our homes. And to make it worse, cigarettes were considered to be good for your nerves! All they were good for, it turned out, was to fatten the manufacturers' purses and blacken our lungs. But back then, who knew?

But bad or good, Walt Pennell's day would be made if he was treated to a bottle of Orange Crush or lime soda, along with a cigarette. He well deserved those few simple pleasures. My heart would certainly buy a carton of those at any price right now if I could have our old Dad back for even a day. The reason for that, of course, is because not a day goes by that I don't kindly think of him and miss him. I'm sure the same is true for many of my siblings.

Being A Kid
In The 1950s

What a wonderful season summer is, and how very wholesome was the daily environment we grew up in! One of our all-time favourite activities in the summer was picking berries. How many times did we, with or without a parent, spend the whole day gathering all types of them from the obliging fields?

The popular spots were over in Soper's Field or the Bakeapple Marsh. Yes, the times were so simple, but how delightful was it to go off on a little excursion with your makeshift containers for all the berries you were excited about picking. You would also happily tote a paper bag containing a few sandwiches that your mother had put together, along with something sweet and a jar of tea, which was put down in a long sock to keep the heat in. If you grew up in Paradise when I did, you'll have the same memories about these summer days, and they are sweet ones to be sure.

Many youngsters cherished a break after bending over for hours on end gathering berries when you would finally sit or lie off in a field. Then you would ravenously open that brown paper bag, devour your picnic lunch and pass around the still-warm bottle of tea - full of sugar and some milk, of course. There wasn't too much worry about spreading germs at those times. Our immune systems were as hearty as that of any horse.

Now a child today, sadly, would have to be accompanied by an adult or an older sibling on an excursion like that. To me, our surroundings seemed idyllic. Maybe we were all too naive about the dangers in society, but happily, we were never the worse for wear because of it. Still, I honestly hope, in my old-fashioned way, that the tradition of children picking berries continues, and that they do go with their containers in tow. That is pretty much all that's required. The days of seeing tables set up along the road with children alongside them yelling, "Blueberries for sale!" seem to have died off. I think the present days of available credit have killed the urgency for earned cash. But when I am lucky enough to occasionally see that sight, it's a sweet step back to my past.

Back in the old days, if a berry-picking trip was even mildly suggested, everyone would scurry home and shortly thereafter leave their house armed with cans or boxes for the berries with their lunch in that brown paper bag or a homemade sack. The next step in the process, and one that will surprise you, was that you would be instructed by a parent or adult to turn your shirt inside out! Remarkably, that made sense to us as children. In addition to that strange rule, you would also have to carry either a crust of bread or a piece of hard tack, which is a hardened cake of bread, in your pockets.

Before you left, you could bet money that you would be sternly warned not to interfere with any mushroom caps and certainly never to kick them over. Why the strange process you ask? The answer to that was simple: to ward off the fairies, of course! The older folks didn't fool around when it came to the fairies, and they definitely made sure that you had an offering of bread in your pockets in case you were ever approached by said fairies. You were sternly warned never, ever to "vex" them by going near their mushrooms. On those berry picking days, I often hoped that they would come after me so I could see what all the fuss was about.

We fondly chuckle at those beliefs now, but generations before us felt quite intimidated by sending children in the woods, for fear of never seeing them again. Apparently, it all stems from Irish myths that were brought over to Newfoundland and spread to all the communities, including Paradise.

As boys, we often ate the bread our mothers had carefully placed in our pockets, tossed it in the bushes for the rabbits, or threw it playfully at each other. Throwing all warnings and caution to the wind, we kicked over our share of mushroom caps, in the hopes of making the little folk confront us. But miraculously, we survived the wroth of all the fairies located in Paradise. We had well tested the rules we were told not to break and had a fair amount of fun while we were violating them. It wouldn't have been advisable, however, to mention that to your parents when you arrived home safely with your shirt still inside out, of course.

Dad would make up cardboard boxes, about one foot by eight inches, lined neatly with wax paper, which he would then sew up with cotton or slight twine. These tidy little containers would fit about a quart or litre of berries, and each box would sell for approximately seventy-five cents to a dollar.

Would we ever be thrilled with the prospect of making some money for the family in late August or September! It could go toward our schoolbooks, school supplies, and clothes for the new school year! We'd stand by the kitchen table, patiently waiting for Mom or Dad to finish lining the boxes and filling them with the various berries but mostly blueberries because they were abundant.

Usually, on this particular adventure, I would be joined by two siblings, Wally and Florie. Armed with two cardboard containers each, we would walk gingerly out the gravel road and down over the steep hill to Topsail Road, cautiously watching the tidy boxes as we walked, so berries wouldn't fall out. We would stand right on the edge of Topsail Road, ever so patiently trying to eagerly catch the attention of every single car and pedestrian who came by. We would broadly smile and yell, "Berries for Sale!" in the hopes that the cars would come to a screeching halt or that a passerby could not resist such sweet and well-behaved children. If you were lucky enough to sell your berries quickly, you would take off back up over Flint Hill, an exercise in itself, and proudly tell Mom or Dad that you needed more as you hurriedly retrieved and showed them the coins in your pockets.

Today, I am amazed at how incredibly steep that hill was and how, as children, we didn't even notice because our priority was to have fun and make a profit. Running up a couple of hills and being out of breath was never a hardship then.

Oh my, what a successful feeling it was to sell four or more of those boxes of berries and to come home with maybe $5 each! There was the odd time we got hungry while trying to anxiously drum up business, and we ate some of our wares. Then, in good conscience, we felt obligated to charge only seventy-five cents. But that was only if you couldn't make the box look full. So, maybe our consciences didn't have a whole lot to do with it!

On our arrival home, we eagerly passed over the remainder of our earnings to one of our parents, and they were put in the pot for everyone's back-to-school needs. Picking blueberries for school expenses was a well-observed tradition in most places on the island. My mother did the same as a child and spent many summer days over on Morrissey's Ridge, which is exactly where Galway, the new development, is located near Mount Pearl.

Like us, my mom and her friends would pack a lunch and, making their way on foot, pick as many berries as possible. They would have a boil-up before returning home. Mom said that they would make the whole day of it and repeat that excursion right through the week, until they had enough berries to cover the upcoming school expenses. Closing your eyelids, you could see blueberries for days.

When we repeated that ritual many years later, if we managed to sell over and above what was expected, we were allowed to visit Gosse's Store, back down over Flint Hill again, for an ice cream or a bottle of 'beer' and a bag of chips. It was worth all the effort to get that treat at the end of the day, after working by the sweat of your brow as a salesman.

How exhilarating it was as a very young child to finish our school year in June and finally be free of books and homework! The very next day, feeling free as the birds, we religiously made a trip to a memorable spot: Mr. Sharpe's Barn, just down the road. Mr. Sharpe deserves a place of honour in my mind, because I did a fair amount of growing up and experienced the total freedom of childhood on his ample property.

As simple an excursion as it was, it was also memorable. Now, while driving past that property, I often recall so many boyhood adventures. In my childhood, though, the whole place looked so much bigger. As youngsters, many of us looked forward to a whole day down Paradise Road, toward St. Philips, to freely play and let our imaginations wander in that old, wonderfully spacious barn.

There would certainly be a bunch of us. Along on that adventure would always be Tommy Sharpe (who luckily was Mr. Sharpe's grandson), Roy Parsons (my cousin), Jackie Lynch, Harvey Janes, and yours truly. Incidentally, Harvey died within the next ten years after battling leukemia. At least that was one solid childhood memory he had to take with him.

Mr. Sharpe didn't mind a bit when we overtook his barn and land. All the children in the area knew that to go in and on his property, we just had to behave and not destroy anything. He would go around performing his chores and let us do our thing. He wasn't the least bit fussy like some other folks in Paradise, and I actually think he enjoyed children being around and being childlike.

Armed with our ample homemade picnic, off we would go for a full day of vacation, playing in the hay or on the cart, pretending to be the best cowboy in the world, the meanest pirate, or our version of a superhero who could do it all in a single bound in such a wonderfully adventurous world.

Looking back, whatever swords, rifles, guns, or bows and arrows we had were ones we had made from sticks gathered in the woods. How many children today, if they pretended to be a cowboy, had an actual real-life horse that they could hop on and pretend was the fastest steed in all the land? The only exception was that we didn't actually ride the horse outside the barn, but that didn't matter. In our young minds we rode it really fast, really hard, and all over the world. We had all that wild imagination at our disposal!

Mr. Sharpe's horse carts never saw as much action during the week as they did when we were jumping from them, at warp speed, like a brave cowboy in the movies. Those carts would also become a store counter, like Mrs. Gosse had in her shop on Topsail Road, and we sold top quality, yet invisible items to our customers. The customers all happened to be about eight years or under, but they paid well with invisible money, and there was always bundles of that. We would wear ourselves out down there doing nothing but letting off a full school year's worth of steam and confusing the animals.

When we had worked up enough of an appetite, fit for a pillaging pirate or bronco-riding cowboy, off we would flop into the various mounds of hay and sit comfortably back with our well-earned brown bag of lunch. You were limited only by your imagination on those memorable and innocent days, and that was never a problem. When you had no store-bought toys, which incidentally we didn't miss a bit, your child's mind produced them with a bunch of branches, and even more whittling. We didn't have any idea how carefree and abundant our lives were at that age, and even though there were no toy departments or arcades to visit, we had something far more vital, and that was creativity, innovation, and determination.

Where would we have been as boys romping around in the 1940s and 1950s if it weren't for utilizing all the lofty trees that surrounded us? They weren't just for swinging or climbing; they were far more useful than that. Did all youngsters on this island, I wonder, make use of their branches like the youngsters in Paradise?

A good-growing tree with big, bushy branches could be magically turned into a work of art, and they were downright multi-purpose items when you were eight or ten years old. How innovative the population was then, when most individuals could turn their hand to at least one item from a tree branch. Not only were actual trees turned into lumber by most of the sawmills around, but branches could be turned into different varieties of brooms or limbed out to make anything from barrels, slides, carts, and even ornaments. Picture, if you will, a chair with a decorative back made by rounding out a tree branch or criss-crossing them for a more elaborate model. We have all seen those.

Years ago, not only in Newfoundland, but in other countries, it was quite a tradition to mark a big public celebration with a decorative arch. If you happen to look at photographs taken before 1950, on an occasion such as a visiting dignitary, you'll often see a tall, ornate arch made totally out of branches.

Some of these arches were absolute works of art, and they were very time-consuming to construct. Some were put together with numerous bushy branches, and others were built using just the wood. I cannot imagine the time spent looking for straight branches for these structures. But one thing was for sure: it wasn't a project everyone could complete. Some of these arches were extremely intricate and required some amount of engineering.

I am very proud to say that one of the finest examples of these decorative arches that were so very popular years ago was built by a neighbour of mine. Mr. Gilbert Lynch was well known for his artistic woodwork as were other members of the Lynch family who lived on Topsail Road, not far from our hill coming up to Paradise. He was well in demand back then, as he was a very talented individual.

One of Mr. Gilbert Lynch's fine decorative wooden arches. He was commissioned to design and build this for a Royal Visit.

In preparation for the royal visit from King George VI to Newfoundland in 1939, Gilbert Lynch was consigned to construct this masterpiece to commemorate the auspicious occasion. The arch was built and placed at Octagon Pond, and as you can see for yourself, it was an impressive design. It was obviously a labour-intensive job for him. Gilbert's reputation for this type of artistic work must have preceded him, or he would never have been considered for such an honourable task.

I didn't come into this world until much later, but I would've been proud as a peacock to be at Octagon Pond that day when Mr. Lynch's arch was on display for all, from miles around, to feast their eyes on. As you can see from the picture, even royalty had to be impressed with that. Not many of us could manage that feat—probably not even the King.

My mother was only a teenager when that celebration took place at Octagon Pond. When she was older and in need of care, I lived with her. She would often reminisce about growing up in Paradise

117

and the people who lived in our area. Even though daily life was challenging, for the most part it was a wonderful time of her life. On several occasions, she proudly recalled and said, "You know, Ches, even the King of England came to Paradise years ago." And she was right because members of the Royal Family did visit Paradise, or at least Octagon Pond on Topsail Road, and that was close enough for Mom.

Yes, sir, in my years on our road in and around Paradise, I've seen so many hand-hewn and beautifully natural things produced from our lofty trees. Men were always in the woods for some reason. Actually "making" things was taken for granted. That's another tradition that's died out, and regrettably so.

If you had a pocketknife or had 'borrowed' your grandfather's axe, you could fashion, among other things, a wonderful bow and arrow for yourself. To be truthful, the string on the bow didn't offer much propulsion, and the arrows were often crooked, but in our minds, it was as fine as anything Robin Hood sported in Sherwood Forest.

Down over Flint Hill on Topsail Road, Gosse's Store sold green fishing line by the foot. If you had managed to find a good branch to make an even better bow, that would mean you were also looking for a way to make some money to buy the line to put on that bow. I remember it costing the outrageous sum of one dime for twenty-five feet of line. It makes me laugh to think about it. How simple and economical were those times.

As vividly as if it was yesterday, I can see Mrs. Gosse inside her general store, which, incidentally, everyone patronized. That fishing line would be held up in her hands and stretched out full across her chest four or five times. There was no such foolishness as half an inch with Mrs. Gosse. She was always generous when it came to stretching that fishing line across her chest.

Mrs. Gosse, I have to say, always served the children in their turn, even if adults entered the shop for provisions that were far more expensive than my bit of fishing line. That gesture, in itself, was a life-learning lesson on how to respect customers and people in general. When the transaction was complete, off you would happily go with the handful of material you needed for your fancy bow and Mrs. Gosse put her solitary dime in the cash register. The deal was done, and you felt pretty special with the adult waiting patiently behind you to be served.

Off we would gallivant, back up over the hill, and tie that thick green line as tightly and as taut as humanly possible to the new bow. Then, off to the woods to find a willing crow! We would find one that was sitting patiently, waiting for us, and ready to meet his Maker. Truth be known, however, our aim or our weapon wasn't very accurate because we didn't manage to kill too many, but we sure frightened flocks of them over those few years.

The most exciting exercise was to line up a row of cans on somebody's fence or any flat surface to see how many we could expertly take down in a row. It was a real competition when you had a few other boys to play with, and there was never a shortage of friends or empty cans to play with on our road. Our needs were certainly simple.

If you had managed to produce a particularly fine bow and arrow, and even if it wasn't the best, it had taken you a considerable while to get it to your liking, so you paid close attention to its where-abouts. Nothing was disposed of too quickly if you had spent time and effort to make it. You also took pride in whatever your hands created, no matter how small or insignificant it may have appeared to someone else.

We couldn't get into any kind of dilemma with fishing poles, however, and we made tons of those. We would find a nice slender branch, limb it out with a pocketknife, and go back down over the hill to Gosse's for more fishing line. You could produce a dandy fishing pole for yourself within the hour. We knew that you could actually buy poles back then, but the thought seemed inconceivable to a child. Wouldn't you have to be awfully rich?

Then we went in search of a cork which would be taken from a rum bottle, mostly, and we would just shove a stick through the cork, put the line around the end of the stick, and apply the cork which, we liked to call our bobber. Once you applied a bent piece of metal for a hook, you were a ready-made fisherman. Then, just like Tom Sawyer, with our pole over our shoulder, and quite often a bite to eat, we were off to try our luck at Neil's Pond on Topsail Road. That area is extremely populated today, but in 1955, it was a real haven for trouters and swimmers.

Even though our rods were pretty rustic and unprofessional, we quite often caught a feed of trout with those handmade poles. I remember it feeling pretty rewarding to catch a few fish with those, as we sat off on the grassy bank in the sunshine, wetting a line in Neil's Pond on a summer's day. We were living the dream and didn't even know it.

I have to insert a story here, because it goes hand in hand with Neil's Pond and our fishing excursions. It's not quite as fairy-tale-like as catching a few trout while you lay off in the sun, but it was an exercise that kept all the boys—before us and since, I'm sure—well entertained.

You'll understand if I'm a little reluctant, however, to mention the immense amount of fun we had with frogs, because it most definitely was a male thing. Any female you reminisce and laugh with about enjoying frogs is horrified at what we used to do, and that includes my own wife, Jan. Here we go, anyway—for all the men out there.

If anyone mentioned Trolley House Meadow in our house, our mother would automatically go into her spiel to discourage you and anyone within hearing distance from venturing anywhere near it.

It was called Trolley House Meadow, incidentally, because there was an actual trolley house placed there next to the tracks. And, of course, it obviously follows that there was a trolley kept in there. Quite often, men from Paradise who were associated with the

Railway would use the trolley to get to work in St. John's if they had no other means of transportation. It had no engine, but it was just one of those machines with the handles on both sides; you used them to accelerate and slow down. It seems pretty antiquated now, but it was a common sight then. Every time I happen to see a silent film with some damsel in distress tied to the train tracks, one of those trolleys appears on the screen, and it joyfully brings me back to that meadow.

A sketch of the exact type of trolley used by men travelling to work in St. John's. It was owned by the Newfoundland Railway but was used by everyone.

Our mother had no problem with the trolley, its house, or even the train tracks. I think she knew that given the opportunity, we would jump aboard and ride that trolley, even though it wasn't allowed for children. I'm not even quite sure if the men who were not employed with the Railway were supposed to use it, but they all did. And, incidentally, so did every boy who grew up in Paradise. How could you not?

But when you happen to be the mother of a huge brood as she was, she knew that she couldn't be everywhere at once. The only fear would be the train coming, and everyone in Paradise, child and adult alike, was used to that. We could hear it coming well off in the distance.

But Florie Pennell firmly believed and warned each and every one of us, with index finger pointing at you, that the swamp area on the other side of this meadow, which was next to Neil's Pond, had no bottom. She would rant and rave that if you went near that swamp, you were as good as dead, and your body would never be found again. That was pretty intimidating to an eight-year-old. So, in order to not directly disobey her, on the odd occasion, we just didn't mention that we were going there. I guess we dealt with the intimidation and fear of it on our way there.

I think Mom would have understood how vitally important it was for us boys to visit that swamp after an afternoon of swimming, fishing, having a picnic, or just generally skylarking. That old boggy swamp was a gold mine to me and my friends because it was chock-full of big, fat, green frogs, and they were just too enticing to pass up. In retrospect, I feel pretty confident that she wouldn't have understood, because women and girls don't like frogs for some reason. All the more reason to go there, we thought.

Into the swamp you would wade, with your shoes and socks thrown on the bank so they wouldn't be soaked when you got home. Your pant legs would be rolled up as far as possible. Then you picked a good spot where you saw frogs jumping or diving, and you stood frozen, not moving an inch, with your eyes glued on the water, and you awaited your target. It took a bit of effort, and some of us fell in, but we would all manage to catch a few slippery frogs.

Now, the question is what do most boys do with frogs? They blow them up with a straw, of course! We would inflate them until they're nice and round and bouncy! They couldn't hop away then, because they were too bloated. Perfect! Off we would go with our puffy frogs. We would put them on the train track and wait patiently for the train to come. Sometimes, we would have close to a dozen frogs sitting there on that track awaiting their demise. When the train passed by, all of us boys would be horrified witnessing that scene, but then we would all fall to the ground laughing until we cried. Mission accomplished.

When I regaled my wife with that little trip down memory lane, her eyes nearly popped out of her head, and she said it was one of the cruellest things she had ever heard. I don't think I'd have the stomach or heart for it now, but back then, it was absolute magic. Who needed TV or fancy toys? Maybe Mom should have been down to the swamp warning the frogs instead of worrying about us.

Along this path called memory lane, I'd have to mention any young boy's all-time favourite, and that would be slingshots. Dozens and dozens of those came out of our surrounding woods as well, much to the dismay of the cows in the fields and the odd screaming girl whom we targeted with it. There were also a couple of old signs around our road that just happened to get more than their share of dents in them. They were stationary and bigger, so they were easier to hit; it was just too tempting for a boy with a slingshot. It was always a fierce competition among the boys to see how many dents we each could inflict in those signs.

Slingshots were really popular items, and they were easy and cheap to come up with. If you found a small V-shaped piece of wood and a thick rubber band, without a doubt, your week was made, and your mischievous side revealed itself. There were rocks aplenty, and they didn't cost a cent.

We never broke anything important with them (that we admitted to, anyway), but they were considered to be a nuisance unless, of course, you were eleven or twelve years old. The downside of those slingshots was the trouble we managed to get into because of them on the odd occasion. Thankfully, that kind of trouble is always temporary—unless, of course, you had inflicted too much of an injury. But the cows weren't complaining. The girls were another matter.

How many of you have seen one of those ships in a bottle? And how many of you have seen how they were put together? There was a man in Paradise by the name of Max Sharpe who made and sold those regularly. My grandfather, Billy Parsons, also was a marvel at creating these unusual gems.

When Grandfather was making one of these boats, I would find any excuse to visit and sat in quiet awe and observed him. He would carefully select the proper pieces of wood and whittle and cut the masts and all the miniature lumber for the construction of his ship. It was painstaking, intricate work, and he was a master at it. You have to consider that there were no craft shops to buy a kit, and it all came from finding your own supplies and making your own. I'd been with him, on occasion, when he would visit one of his friends' sawmills and pick up a few desired pieces.

If you happened to notice Grandfather in the woods behind his or our house studying the branches, you knew there was a ship in the works. He would size up a bend in a tree branch to see how much work it would take to obtain the result he needed for the little lumber. The fresher the branch, the easier it was to manipulate. Now, that's what I call starting from scratch.

He would whittle and sand down the various parts and lay them all out gently on the table in his kitchen, and then he was ready for assembly. The trick to these, of course, is that the ship is constructed outside, and not inside, the bottle. I have witnessed people staring at those bottles, and you can read the confusion on their face as to how the tall ship got in there. I would have been one of them if I hadn't seen it done first-hand.

To get his bottle ready, he would insert what looked like putty on the side, where the ship would eventually be positioned. With a flat knife or stick, he would flatten the putty until he knew it was well stuck and wouldn't waiver. Following that, he would insert a long, thin paint brush, similar to those used by artists. With that brush, he would paint the sides of the putty with a little white paint, which would really resemble rough waves and some blue paint similar to the colour of the sea.

If he wanted the sails to look unfurled, as opposed to tied to the mast, he would have to make each individual sail. They would probably be cut from soft, thin leather. That leather was easily obtained because a lot of people patched their own shoes and boots. Dad, being our own cobbler, always had pieces of leather lying around.

Another way to create a sail was from plain brown paper. Those would then be attached to thin pieces of wood representing the mast. And the different sails would be connected to each other and the ship with string or slight twine. These miniature masts would be attached to the body of the ship with a hinge. He would often fashion those hinges himself out of pieces of wire. Therein lies the mystery of how the ship is in the bottle! With the beauty of the hinge, the masts with their sails could be lowered outside the bottle, inserted into the neck, and then those strings would be pulled up, one by one, outside the bottle, making the sailing vessel stand tall *inside* the bottle. I used to love to be there for that part of the process. It was seeing an actual launching.

His next job was to apply a dab or two of glue with a long thin stick, just inside the neck of the bottle. Then, with a tiny tweezer-type tool, he would tenderly hold that string, position it just over the glue, and ensure that the mast was straight before gingerly attaching the string to the glue. He patiently waited for that string to take hold in the glue because, as he told me once, as I watched, "if that string lets go after you cut it, your sails will never go up." When Grandfather was confident that the masts could stand on their own, he would cut off the excess string.

It was extremely impressive to watch him as he squinted at the small, intricate little pieces, and through experience, he knew exactly where every part should be placed. If it was a three-master with sails supposedly down, twine would be wrapped around each mast in order for it to represent that. The long strings would be tied to each mast which was again on a hinge awaiting insertion into the bottle.

I know that this talented old man didn't charge a quarter of what those ships were worth. It's quite an understatement to say that those professionally handmade works of art were labour-intensive. You could feel his passion for making them as you sat by him, listened, and observed. I so regret that I don't have one as a keepsake in honour of his hard work, the time spent with him, and his unlimited patience.

All that being said, though, the first-place winner of the most popular item that came out of the Paradise woods were, without a doubt, the hockey sticks! During the winter, you would make a concentrated effort to take your time while you trudged through the wet, snowy woods to find just the right length and shape of the branch. With eyes scouring each tree, once you found the perfect branch, you would simply saw it or break it off. With tender loving care, attention, and lots of elbow grease, you could manufacture yourself a replica of a hockey stick. We would even endeavour to put a curve on the blade, like we knew the professional hockey players had, but most times the curve wasn't quite as professional as we would have liked it. Or, to be brutally honest, the curves never did work out, but we pretended they were first-rate. The best stick ever!

But if you wanted it to be a really special, looked-like-the-real-thing stick, off you would trot to my other grandfather, Jim Rixon, who lived just next door. One thing that is definitely true about getting older is that experience is a wonderful teacher. Both of my grandfathers seemed to be able to put their hand to just about anything. They both came from a time, like most older people back then, when Canadian Tire and Walmart didn't exist. If you needed something, you usually made it yourself. And making fantastic sticks was a gift that Jim Rixon possessed. Honestly, when I was nine and ten years old and he presented me with one of his hockey sticks, I felt that it was worthy of playing the Stanley Cup. And his sticks were all home-grown and locally manufactured, to boot.

Sadly, the sticks we quickly whittled and sanded ourselves were no match for ones produced by Grandfather Rixon. The ones I came up with myself usually broke off before the first period was over during our games on Neil's Pond. So, what's a would-be hockey hero to do? You played the remainder of the game with whatever was left of the stick, of course, and just hoped that you got really lucky or that the goalie on the opposing team wasn't very athletic. I can remember playing hard at one game with no blade at all, but just the straight stick, and actually scoring with it! It was obvious that we were too young (or just too enthusiastic) to worry about impressing anyone with the proper gear.

And with hockey came skates. We didn't offer the NHL suppliers much competition, but nowhere would you find as many varieties of skates as our young population had. There was the type made from pieces of cardboard tied to your feet with a piece of rope or twine—they were very slippery if nothing else, unless the cardboard got wet. Then they literally dissolved before your eyes. However, if you had more cardboard, then you could have more skates. We weren't easily deterred.

Some more creative kids would endeavour to sharpen a branch loosely resembling a skate blade, with a few inches on either end of the "blade" to work into the cardboard. Then they would tie those to their feet via string or rope wrapped around their ankle. Those were a little time-consuming, though, and they didn't last. You were good to go for a while, sliding on that particular brand of skate until the wood on the bottom cracked, which it always did. Then you were back to the cardboard variety, which was already on your feet. If nothing else could be said about what we didn't have, let it be loudly proclaimed that Paradise children possessed a healthy supply of optimism.

Tex Janes (my cousin) and I came across an abandoned but real pair of skates one time. It had real blades. What a tremendous find! I remember that it was later in the day, and dusk was just approaching.

We couldn't believe our amazing luck as we quickly scurried to a little pool of ice that had formed in a field between Tex's house and Gordon Janes' store.

We were so young at the time that Tex's mother, Aunt Jen, wouldn't let us go to a pond by ourselves. So, that mini pool had to do. We eagerly cleared anything on the ice in record time and put these marvels on, switching back and forth, taking turns at five- to ten-minute intervals. It was only the two of us, so we didn't have to take turns with half the boys in Paradise, which would've been the case had we been detected.

The only hitch in our exciting find was that one skate was size 5, and the other size 8. No problem. The size 5 was just a little taut to get on, and the size 8 required a couple of socks stuffed into the toe. We didn't have extra socks with us, I recall, so when Tex skated, I took off my socks and lent him and, vice versa when I skated. It was piercing cold to sit there, cross-legged on the ice, without socks, and your mitts holding your feet as you waited your turn, but what the heck—we had skates!

They felt a little unusual on our feet when we managed to actually stay upright, but that didn't really matter because the fact remained that we had real blades, and we were ecstatic. What was there to complain about?

My only regret was that after that winter, we didn't keep those odd skates. What a great conversation piece they would make now, hung up and tied together, one brown and one black, and two significantly different sizes. When I finally did get my own skates, it was wonderful, but they didn't offer much of a challenge like the old ones.

If you lived up our way, you could never forget the brisk, moonlit winter nights lighting up our ever-popular Flint Hill before streetlights were installed and ruined it all. It was so very pretty that I can close my eyes and still revel in the sight. We would skate and slide down over it until we wore ourselves out. No one needed a gym membership then. You ate what you were given at your meals, and you worked it off, either by work or play.

There was no traffic to interfere with our fun, but if there was the odd motorist on Topsail Road, there was always some child at the bottom of the hill to yell, "Car!" All paused until the "traffic" passed, and the games continued. There was never a serious accident, thankfully, but the odd pedestrian was made a little frazzled while walking home from work and trying to make their way up the hill without colliding with one of us on the way down.

Now, I seriously don't remember any child in Paradise owning an actual store-bought slide, but then again, slides came in various forms. If you were desperate for a slide, there was your ever-popular tree branch, the bushier the better, but always the last resort; a cardboard box, or at least a good-sized piece of one; a wooden panel from anything found in the shed; a hand slide usually used for work in the woods; a shovel to sit on; or an abandoned car bonnet or car door. There were also those greased-lightning round washer tops.

Remember the wringer washers that came with a round metal top to go over the tub? Some brave souls would sneak their washer top out of their house without their mother knowing. I would not have ever been that brave or silly. If you lost that and were found out, you wouldn't be able to sit on a slide or anything else for a week. Interfering with a woman's washer was serious stuff. But if you did manage to acquire one of those metal tops, you were in for one fast ride, albeit a really unpredictable one. They would spin around and around as you went down over the hill because they were impossible to control or steer. And you really never knew where you would end up or how your stomach would feel once you got there. Most times, you would rely on your friends to stop you before you slid into anything important and killed yourself—like a car, a horse, or God forbid, your mother looking for the top of her washer.

As for the car doors or bonnets, the older boys would somehow commandeer these various parts with pieces of metal sticking out of them from every angle. They weren't exactly factory-approved items and dangerous to even look at. I guess that was half the fun. There would often be some car wrecks around our area and you could easily help yourself to a piece of it. You would, however, normally do that when no one was looking which was the unspoken law regarding those particular slides.

Other times, the car parts looked in remarkably good shape, and I was always curious about where the lads had confiscated them. On reflection, I amusingly wonder if a car owner down on Topsail Road may have gone out to his car one winter's morning to find a door missing. This would be something similar to a hen owner counting his or her hens after a local card game!

And we weren't to miss out on a little night-time mischief either. On school nights, when dusk came and your chores and homework were done, we ran out the door to go sliding on Flint Hill. But after an hour, you could set your clock by a certain older female resident who lived right on the hill and shall remain nameless. Out she would creep to the road, muttering to herself, lugging a heavy pail of ashes, and throw it over the snow right where we would slide. Her hope was that we would be encouraged to give up in despair and go home—or have to face our parents with our clothes covered from head to toe with soot.

However, going home rarely happened if your mother wasn't calling for you for the third time. So, once again, out came the tree branch, and we would whisk most of the ashes off the hill and jump on our slides for just a couple of more slides. That was always to this poor woman's dismay, though, because she would go to phase two and yell, "You boys should all be gone home hours ago!"

I often wondered why this woman was so contrary about a few children having a bit of fun in the snow. It must've been pretty quiet in her house, I used to think, if our yells and laughter annoyed her to that extent. I know that in our house, you could barely hear yourself think at any given hour. Hearing outside noises in our home was impossible.

When I got my driver's licence years later, I found, like most motorists in the area, that because the children had beaten down the snow into what was now shiny ice with the continuous sliding and skating, driving up over that icy grade would be next to impossible. That was before the fancy trucks we have now, with all kinds of traction, and before sanders came up our way. Perhaps that was the lady's problem, listening to the hopeless screech of the scattered vehicles' tires trying to make it up over Flint Hill while she was trying to settle in comfortably for the night.

Every once in a while, if we had zipped down and walked up with our slides once too often, our tired little bodies would give into her wishes once her ash bucket appeared. Then we would retreat and make for our homes, rosy-cheeked, weary, wet, and incapable of feeling our feet from the cold. But we were content.

As mentioned above, as normal boys, we weren't beyond the realm of creating our own brand of harmless mischief. There was the odd Halloween, when, dressed in outrageous creations that we managed to fashion together from old shirts, pants, blouses, and hats from our parents' closets, we managed to find a little devilment for ourselves.

If we visited a house, knocked on the door, and discovered that there were no treats distributed by this household, that would be a downright sacrilege. To make matters even worse at a few houses, you would be sternly and loudly chastised and driven away with nothing but a disappointed face. Unbelievably, a few of these people were relatives of ours.

Well, it just didn't seem fair or proper for adults—and certainly relations—to refuse to pass out a few candies to us, or at least be civil on Halloween. So, we maturely decided that if they didn't treat, we would trick!

Giving it lofty consideration for about a minute or less, my brother Herb, cousins Len and Roy Parsons, Tommy Sharpe,

Dawson Newman, and I, concluded that the just punishment for this unwarranted meanness would be to quietly and carefully climb to the top of that particular person's roof. Armed with a couple of really heavy, damp sods that we had pulled out of an obliging field, we would scamper to the back of the house. Whispering our plans among ourselves, we would decide who the best candidate was to levy the punishment. One of us, and oftentimes it would be me, would get a boost up to the roof. Luckily for us, most houses in Paradise at the time were one storey.

Some of the cousins I grew up with. L-R: Jack and Lester Rixon,

Cousin Amelia (Parsons) Reid.

Mrs. Locke and my cousin, Len Parsons.

I remember that I was selected to be the culprit one time, being perhaps the lightest weight to boost up. Once up there, I tiptoed as noiselessly as possible across the roof and gently laid those sods, totally covering the chimney. As quick as lightning striking, I jumped down from the roof, we all made a hasty retreat out the lane, and we crouched down outside their gate to watch the anticipated havoc.

We knew from previous experience that the desired result would take less than two or three minutes. As we excitedly looked on, waiting for the sods to do their work, the miserly inhabitants would come shrieking out of a smoke-filled house, waving their fists and shouting many enthusiastic choice words at us. The home-made masks we had with us were a godsend as we watched the whole fiasco unfold.

A good portion of the yelling was to tell us that they knew who we were and that our parents would well know tomorrow what delinquents they had raised. Whether they knew us or actually informed our parents, we never heard anything after that Halloween. We were blessed that we were never recognized or told on each other. After a few years of similar tricks, most houses gave out treats. I don't know if they were afraid or if they just got friendlier.

Sometimes, climbing up roofs or tearing up sods seemed like too much of a job. Consequently, our bag of tricks also included the old gate switch trick. Believe it or not, some people would give you one single candy or tell you they were "shelled out," which meant they had given everything away. We knew, however, that some households were shelled out before Halloween even started. They just didn't recognize the occasion.

If we bothered to walk up two lanes, to two different houses, and knock on two doors of people who gave us nothing, we knew that it was our responsibility to take one person's gate and switch it with the other miserable person's gate at the end of their lanes. And that often happened.

You wouldn't believe what hard work it is, lifting those gates out of place and lugging them up and down the road. The boys and I would huff and puff under the laborious weight of it all, especially if you're ten and weigh less than a hundred pounds. But the effort and the sweat were well worth it once the job was done. I sit here and smile as I realize that we were indeed a devilish lot, but that was about as much damage as we inflicted... If you don't count the sods episodes, the frogs, and the slingshots.

One day after Halloween, my father came in the house at suppertime and calmly asked us boys if we knew anything about what happened to the gates owned by Mr. Garland and Mr. Murphy. We didn't have the heart to lie to Dad, so we just stood there, eyes downcast and didn't speak. He knew full well that it was us by our guilty faces, but Dad being the meek and quiet type he always was just said, "Well, if it was ye, you shouldn't be at that, boys." And that was that.

Our Dad never raised a hand to us at any time, and I guess that would be the time to do it if he was any way inclined. Probably, he had struggled with a few gates himself in his youth. He was quiet, yes, but he had been a young boy at one point too.

Walter Pennell was never one to cause much of a fuss, inside or outside the house, and we knew that we had a whole year to recover from the guilt, just in case we were provoked again next October. At the time, just switching a few old gates seemed like a fitting retribution to demonstrate how unfair it was to deny a child a treat at Halloween.

At my age, I should feel ashamed for making those poor old men climb up on their roofs, when the cold winds of winter were howling around them, in order to get rid of the sods covering their chimneys. I should also feel guilty for forcing them out on the road to look feverishly for their misplaced gates. But, hey, I'm not harbouring any bad feelings, and those incidents always make me chuckle with satisfaction.

Our First Attempt At
Making Moonshine

Why is it that when you're young, you want to do everything an adult does? Some projects should never be attempted when you're young and inexperienced, and one of those is definitely making moonshine. That job is for the pros!

Now, as any Newfoundlander knows, as pretty an orange colour as dogberries are, they are never really in demand for anything edible and would certainly never be picked for a dessert recipe. But one attribute to their credit is that they are surely plentiful, especially given our harsh winters. They're also a source of nourishment for the poor birds in the winter when everything else is covered with snow. Still, I'm sure that if the birds had their "sooners," they wouldn't eat them either!

When I was an adolescent, maybe twelve or thirteen years old, I entered somewhat adult territory with an attempt at making moonshine. Joining me in this adventurous task were my cousins, Tex, Harvey, and Victor Janes; another cousin, Roy Parsons; and my friend who lived next door, Tommy Sharpe.

We decided that it was high time that we tried our hand at making our own moonshine in the form of dogberry wine. After all, we were nearly thirteen! Now, the fact of the matter was that none of us had ever tasted wine before, and none of us had certainly ever tried to make any kind of wine before. But we had always heard the older folks in the community when they'd say that the dogberries were ripe enough now to make a batch. So, we listened attentively until we heard our elders mention the dogberries again, and then we felt the time was right.

Being the confident, young bucks we were, we were determined to come up with a batch of dogberry wine that would be superior to any hootch that ever came out of Paradise. There was no doubt in our young, foolish minds that we would make it perfectly the first time around.

Our first plan of attack after the berries were picked from the trees was to raid each of our mother's pantries for the yeast that was required. We didn't know how much yeast, exactly, but when you are twelve or thirteen, that fact seems incidental. We retrieved, on the sly, a huge double boiler that belonged to one of my aunts. We heaved all the berries that we could fit in there, along with gallons of water, and proceeded to mash the berries as well as we could. The boys and I were aware that you had to let it sit and ferment for a while, but again, we didn't know exactly how long it took, and we were afraid to inquire in case we would be found out. However, we were positive that we weren't going to waste time waiting too long for the end product.

I can remember that it felt very adult to be brewing our own stuff; precisely and properly carrying out the process was an afterthought. One fact that was glaringly obvious, however, was that we weren't allowed to be making moonshine in the first place, which made it even more exciting. I think that I would much rather have been caught by the authorities and handcuffed than caught by my mother for making moonshine. She would have skinned me alive, and there would never be another batch on her watch. However, we were boys, and we were anxious to try our hand at making liquor—and even more importantly, to drink it.

So, with the double boiler full of mashed berries, yeast, and water, we hurriedly sneaked down the road trying to look inconspicuous while looking behind us every step of the way. And believe me, two adolescent boys trudging down the road, each holding a handle of a double boiler, is conspicuous enough. Two other boys right behind them whispering to each other and looking in all directions is a real red flag. I wonder if any older adults looked out their window and laughingly said, "Looks like the boys are going to try their hand at making a drop of shine." Probably so.

We brought our stash to the barn owned by friendly Mr. Sharpe. He really didn't know what we were up to, and we could come and go as we liked, as long as we were respectful of him and his property. Every day, we would gallivant down to Mr. Sharpe's, checking on the progress of the ripening berries, as if we could recognize the signs.

We had the boiler discreetly hidden under the hay in the loft. I remember climbing quickly up to that loft and eagerly lifting the lid to inspect our brew. One day, not too much later, cousin Tex Janes and I, went down to the barn and were thrilled to death when we opened the lid and convinced ourselves that it smelled like it had worked. In Newfoundland, the word "worked" has a double meaning; in this instance, it meant the berries were fermenting and turning into liquor. I doubt very much that was the case, but when you happen to be thirteen, you can convince yourself of anything.

The next step of our operation was to pour the mixture into all the Purity Syrup bottles and old rum or whisky bottles we could come up with. I know for a fact that we thought it unnecessary to sterilize or even wash the bottles—unless, of course, we had found then in a ditch. In that case, we gave the bottles a little run under the tap when no one was looking.

The elixir was an odd-looking one, with some of the berries still intact and covered in foam from the yeast. But carefully, we managed to divide it up among the bottles. Without being able to ask advice from anyone, we had all previously agreed that two weeks should be sufficient time for our batch to ferment. Of course, we were horribly wrong on that count. It was more likely that two weeks was about all the patience we could muster to wait for the results.

Well, when all was said and done, the whole ordeal was a one-time only venture. It was time ill spent, and the results were less than satisfactory. In fact, they were disastrous. You wouldn't think it humanly possible to make dogberries taste worse than they naturally are, but we were successful in that for sure.

We were more than fortunate, looking back, that the whole contents of the boiler didn't explode with the huge helpings of yeast we added. It lifted the lid of the boiler, alright, but chances are that it could have lifted the roof of poor Mr. Sharpe's barn had we left it the proper length of time for fermentation. Thank God we were anxious.

I am sure that one of us must have overheard the old folk mention that dogberry wine required an awful lot of sugar, but do you think we remembered that small ingredient? Of course, we didn't. So, the anxious day came when our anticipation got the better of us. We just had to sample our one-of-a-kind special blend of dogberry wine, which was still in berry form for the most part, and still covered in mounds of frothy yeast and water.

Off we all anxiously and suspiciously trotted down the road to Mr. Sharpe's barn for the big unveiling of our brew. None of the family knew where we were going, but I felt like everyone we met could read the intention on our guilty faces. Our consciences persevered, though, and we climbed the loft and made ourselves comfortable. Sitting in the hay, we proudly passed around the first sample of our own special brew in the long-necked Purity Syrup bottle.

I can still see the boys' faces as they took their first taste. Such screwed up, gruesome faces you never saw before. When the Purity

Syrup bottle came to me, I took a huge mouthful and understood immediately why the other boys looked as they did. I was tempted to spit it out, but that would admit failure, and I knew that wasn't going to happen.

Managing to finally gulp down the vile stuff, we all enthusiastically insisted it must be really strong moonshine because it was so very awful. We even convinced ourselves that we were becoming a little drunk from it. We were delighted that we had accomplished such an adult undertaking and happily and unanimously agreed, when we got our faces to stop twitching, that it was "some good stuff."

But in fact, we weren't at all drunk, and it was, without the shadow of a doubt, the most awful concoction I ever put to my lips. When we decided that we had sampled enough of our home brew, we threw it in the bog just down from the house. I honestly don't think even the bog deserved that crucifixion. It probably dried up all that area overnight.

We didn't admit it to each other, but I think we each knew that we had better eavesdrop a little closer to the local professionals before we attempted a second batch. As we have gotten older, we chuckle whenever we reminisce about that wonderful batch of dogberry wine we produced. I did often wonder afterwards if we had all our mothers puzzled as they stood in their pantries back then scratching their heads and saying to themselves, "I'm sure I bought more yeast than that." I never did divulge that venture to Mom, and I'm also sure it wasn't the first time she missed items out of her pantry.

Where To Go And
What To Do: Coming Of Age In Paradise

Spring and summer were generously welcomed every year, if only because the snow was melted, and the temperatures were finally starting to rise. It was then that we took it upon ourselves to venture a little further down our quaint little country road to the busier Topsail Road area. If you were inclined to relax and treat yourself on a Sunday afternoon in the summer, you had the choice of Neil's Pond or Octagon Pond for a boisterous swim and skylarking in and out of the water with your friends.

In the 1950s, Octagon Pond was quickly taking on the grand appearance of a sporting resort. Different varieties of sailboats and rowboats were continuously on the pond and in frequent use. There was even a boathouse there. This seemed really high-class to us, given that some of the little houses on the road where we lived weren't much bigger than this boathouse.

It was a very common occurrence to see seaplanes landing and taking off in Octagon Pond. Cars driving along Topsail Road would often pull in and watch a plane land or take off. My wife tells me that she remembers her father pulling in there to admire the planes as her family made its way out of town.

We would stand there as if frozen, on the edge of Octagon Pond, anxiously waiting for a circling plane to make a landing on the water with its pontoons. It was thrilling to watch, and it was a big deal to see a seaplane that closely. We would wait and watch the pilot get out, and we all figured that this man must have been very smart and very rich to be flying a plane. We were probably wrong on both counts, but you would never convince us otherwise then.

All of the congested traffic, pedestrian or motorized, around that area bolstered business at the Park Le, which was a catering hall and restaurant right on the edge of Octagon Pond. The building that housed the Park Le became the popular Pinewood in the 1980s, which catered to all kinds of events. That building housed a couple of extremely prosperous businesses over the years, and it wasn't demolished until just a few years ago. There was also the well-frequented convenience store known as Shute's, which sold quite a few ice-cream cones and Cokes on weekend afternoons. That building still stands today, just across the street from Octagon Pond, and it is now a Marie's Store.

If you came down over Flint Hill onto Topsail Road, turned left, and travelled about one kilometre, you could treat yourself to the best fish and chips on the Avalon Peninsula. And that establishment, which I've mentioned earlier, was the famous Soper's, owned and operated by James Soper. Even the townies would make the eight- to ten-mile excursion to come and devour Mr. Soper's fish and chips.

My friends and some of my brothers and sisters would often spend hours in the evening in that big, white, one-storey building. We sat at the counter on the red, round high stools. Soper's was where you would catch up on all the news and gossip; where you would trade ideas and make deals on cars and car parts; and where you kept an eye on that pretty girl who was often there as you waited on your fish and chips with gravy and dressing.

Walking in, you would often meet patrons leaving with their orders in cardboard trays wrapped in wax paper and a brown paper bag with the beautiful aroma of dark cider vinegar. I can smell it now. No matter when you last ate, there was always room for their fish and chips.

Soper's had the reputation of being the "best feed" in or out of St. John's. Their chips were second to none after coming out of that deep fryer.

At their gas bar, which was on the same property, you could buy all kinds of treats. That idea was brand new back then, because gas stations sold exactly what the name implies—gas—and tire gauges or fan belts. The person behind the counter where you paid for your gas was covered in black grease from working on cars. Gas stations with every convenience known to man didn't become a thing until the mid 1970s.

The building that housed that gas bar and confectionery still stands today, operating as a fish and chip restaurant called the Cod Father.

Moving on to the nighttime haunts, we continuously sought an opportunity, especially with puberty well underway, to seek the company of the opposite sex, whether it was inside Soper's or not. We were all single and curious. It was such a glorious, carefree time when your biggest concern in life was whether you had enough money for a bite out and maybe a Coke.

In our Livingroom, L-R: my brother, Lock; Jack Fisher, Doris (last name unknown),
Una (Tilley) Pennell, and her husband, my brother Herb.

Some of my favourite nights were had in what were commonly referred to as "honky-tonks," which was the terminology we used then. It doesn't sound too wholesome, but these lively spots certainly were all the rage with their jukeboxes and pinball machines. And they actually were wholesome for teenagers.

If my memory serves me correctly, and if you're in my age range, the popular spots for me were probably the same for you. There was Martin Lawlor's on the St. Thomas Line, Pender's in St. Philips, Westcott's, which was just west of Soper's Store, Hussey's in Topsail, and Daisy's in Foxtrap.

At these wonderful and much-patronized establishments, you would spend half your night trying to beat the score of the guy ahead of you at pinball and the other half trying to score with the ladies. Most of the ladies were probably fourteen or fifteen, and you were perhaps the tender age of sixteen yourself.

These honky-tonks were extremely popular with our age group, and you could depend on ample company and some frivolous fun to be enjoyed. But actually getting to where the honky-tonks and the girls were could be a chore if you didn't have access to a car.

I started driving lessons with my father at the experienced age of seven, at which time I couldn't reach the pedal or the clutch. While sitting on Dad's lap as we drove down Paradise Road, I would straighten out my left leg and push in on the clutch as Dad changed the gears, saying to me, "That's it, you're doing it." I may have been Grade Two at the time. I thought that I was driving that car for sure, and I couldn't wait to totally take over the driver's seat. Unfortunately, I had to wait a few more years and a few more inches before he let me take his car out on my own. I actually did start driving at thirteen. Red tape wasn't so bright red back then, and many people drove without licences or insurance. I wouldn't recommend it, but that practice was quite common back in the 1950s and 1960s. There weren't too many police cars patrolling our roads either, which worked to our youthful benefit.

There was an occasion in the early 1960s when I was the proud owner of a 1957 Dodge. It was white on top and green on the bottom. This beauty was all restored inside and out, and it was definitely girlfriend ready. I had paid all of fifty-five dollars for it! The only thing missing was seatbelts, and no one ever used those back then, even if they were installed in your car. That was well before the law enforced any safety regulations.

By the time six or eight of my buddies or siblings squeezed in for the ride down to Martin's or Pender's, my fancy rig was looking the worse for wear. I suppose you could say that these places were within walking distance, but walking distance back then could mean ten kilometres. But by car, truck, thumb, or foot, by hook or by crook, we were determined to get there, and we always did. When you're a fifteen- or sixteen-year-old boy, your hormones tend to be quite the driving force as you step out to try the world on for size.

I can well remember those lean years as a teenager when you would have a date and maybe one solitary dollar in your pocket, which you would spend on her. Sometimes, after spending that dollar, you would lose her to someone else; at other times, it got you a kiss. Maybe some of the girls were wise enough to wait for their treat before they made eyes at someone else. That didn't happen too often to me, I have to say, but one time when it did, I was tempted to ask her for my money back. But it was all part of the new experience for us, and you dealt with it. Suffice to say she didn't get the second dollar!

A Browning Harvey truck making a delivery outside one of my favourite honky-tonks.

At the time, we didn't realize how invaluable these places were in terms of learning how to socialize, converse, listen and compete. And we often did compete for the attention of that cute girl who went there and who, unfortunately, had also caught the attention of several of your peers. You learned, in short, how to grow up. Those honky-tonks were your opportunity to have a dance, mix with people your own age, make a new friend, make a bad friend and learn how to deal with him, play an exciting game of pinball, and share a bottle of Spur with your old friends. You could learn how to land a girlfriend or get yourself in a pickle by landing someone else's girlfriend, which is clearly not advisable.

I witnessed a couple of rowdy incidents outside these honky-tonks. Two boys would come to blows over the charms and attention of a certain female, and it usually resulted in a black eye for one of them. It must be a male thing, but we all loved standing around watching and yelling during a good fight. We always had our hopes hung on one guy. These fistfights never lasted very long, and for the most part, they weren't very violent. The other girls, however, would invariably disappear when a disruption started, or they would stay on the fringe of the crowd to see how desperately the girl in question was wanted.

In my mind's eye, I can still see the bright lights flashing on those pinball machines and hear the continuous pings when someone would pull on the lever just right and make a good shot. It was just so much clean and innocent fun with ample camaraderie shared there. We all won a few hearts, and we had them broken along the way, too.

We saw good behaviour as well as bad, and we decided what route we would take. We learned consideration and the perks of reciprocation. The owners of these establishments were not rich people, and we also learned to respect them and their property.

Had we all known, looking back, that those now memorable days would ultimately come to an end, we would've stayed longer and had an extra game of ping pong or two. But for the Paradise teen, life and time marched on, as it did for the rest of the planet, and we had to march with it.

Paradise's
"Characters"

What would our world be without colour? What adds that colour to our wonderful world? When it comes to a community, it would be the people who live in it. I grew up thinking that I was related to every older woman in Paradise because we called them all 'Aunt.' However, it turns out that wasn't the actual reality at all. Because all of us were so familiar with the inhabitants of Paradise through visiting each other's houses and going to school, it certainly felt like family, and most residents were regarded as such.

Paradise was so small back then. There was just one main road. Of course, when it came to the overall population, we had every personality type imaginable. We had the good and the not-so-good, the generous and the stingy, the lovable and approachable types, and the poor souls who never cracked a smile. There were hard workers who toiled from dawn to dusk and some too lazy to breathe, people who pilfered on a regular basis and those who'd give you the shirt off their backs. There were academic types who could quote the odd verse of Shakespeare and artistic types who could create outstanding things out of nothing. There were great relationships between husbands and wives, and there were also secretive affairs, children born from them, and all the gossip that naturally ensued from that. In other words, we lived in a normal environment.

Oscar Wilde: 19th century Irish poet and playwright, summed it up perfectly in his quote, "Be yourself, everyone else is already taken." That clearly speaks of some of the wonderful, yet unusual characters that lived among us.

I was happy to know one small but dynamic individual in my youth. I have already mentioned this gentleman, who was fondly known as Joey Roundboy. Yes, Roundboy! Now, Joey's real surname was Lynch, and how he acquired that peculiar nickname is unknown. I've inquired about his name over the years, but am usually met with a hunch of the shoulders, which indicates that no one knows. I really regret not having asked him the origin of his nickname. Contrary to what a reader may surmise from the name, he was the smallest, thinnest little creature that God ever created. He stood about 5'4", weighed all of a hundred and thirty pounds, and was a quiet, mellow fellow. His nose was long and pointy, and he always wore a quiff hat. Unfortunately, he suffered from severe vision problems.

Joey was the official Justice of the Peace for Paradise, and he was regarded by all around as an educated and intelligent man. If there was an important 'paper' that needed to be legally authorized, Joey was your man. On many occasions in my youth, I had the task of running to his house, which was just down the road from ours, with an important paper clutched in my hand. I would actually have to point to the line that required his signature, and I'm sure that most times, he wasn't aware of what he had signed, even though he held the document an inch from his face. I would watch carefully and with much curiosity as he applied that embossed seal to the document that I had given him. Somehow, any document's importance seemed to triple once Joey put his hand to it.

When we visited Joey, we mostly looked forward to the variety of animals in and around his kitchen. There were the regular cats and dogs, and oftentimes the odd goat. His dimly lit, old-fashioned kitchen was built so that the rafters were exposed, and his hens and rooster would live there. If you think about it, it's not often—even back then—that you would visit a person in their home and have to keep looking up for the location of a bird of any kind. But we kept a vigilant eye to the hens' droppings, as they often rudely relieved themselves from their lofty perches.

I don't think making it to the cover of *Good Housekeeping* magazine was high on Joey's list of priorities. It was much to his benefit that his wife kept a somewhat watchful eye on all the little creatures coming and going. I'm glad, in a way that the poor, old fellow actually couldn't see well, because his floor, counters, and even his kitchen table were, at times, quite the mess. Remarkably, they didn't poison themselves, because they always appeared at the peak of health. Bird droppings notwithstanding, Joey was a fine, old soul. Of course, it was great sport for boys, and you'd be absolutely delighted and ready to burst with laughter if your brother got "hit." What was even more delightful was that your brother couldn't react until we got outside. It made for the best of antics going home—unless, of course, you were the target. Oh, boys, may they never change!

Joey was also the owner and operator of a local sawmill. Curiously, he operated all the machinery in that mill without incident. As a youngster visiting his sawmill, I watched him in amazement and awe as he, with the saw at full throttle, cut a piece of lumber in two. The only difference with Joey was that he couldn't actually see that piece of lumber. He would only know that the wood was totally spliced when the tip of his quiff hat, which he had strategically placed to touch the wood as it fed through, would stop vibrating. I always felt anxious watching him; I was afraid that he would make a mistake, but he never did while I was around. He would assume that bent-over position, hat touching the wood, for each log that fed through.

It's incredible that he never lost a finger—and luckily for Joey, he never lost that hat.

This fine little gentleman represented Paradise in a nutshell. If there was a way to better our lives there, he would strive to do just that. It was through Joey's own initiative that a Government grant was acquired for the improvement of our roads. My brother, Lock, and a dozen other older local boys were given jobs to improve our roads and rid them of potholes. Joey might not have been blessed with eyesight, but that never presented a shortcoming to him.

Now, Joey was married to Julia who was fondly called "Jul" by the populace of Paradise. She stood a good foot or so taller than Joey, but that never seemed to interfere with their happiness. Their marriage produced no offspring, but that never seemed to be an issue either. They always seemed to be continuously busy and productive otherwise.

Julia (Jul) Lynch, crouched down between her Rixon nieces,
Evelyn, Mildred, and Libby (L-R).

The first thing you would recall if you thought of Jul was her unusual attire. I honestly don't remember one day, winter or summer, Sunday or weekday, that Jul didn't wear her rubber boots. Nothing too strange about that, says you? Well, they were knee-length rubber boots, and every day of her life, she would wear a dress with them.

Jul had a variety of knee-length multi-coloured dresses but just one precious pair of rubber boots. Apparently, she thought they matched everything. It seemed normal to all of us at the time to see tall Jul traipsing up the road in those things during every season. I distinctly remember a childhood afternoon when I studied her and wondered whether those boots came off at bedtime. She worked for about ten years at the Birch Plant on Topsail Road and walked to and from there every day, spending her work shift and the remainder of her day in those heavy boots.

In my memory, Jul was known as a cordial and kind old soul. But apparently, she could also be crusty, if not a little eccentric at work; she was definitely not one to cross. A friend of mine who worked with Jul at the Birch Plant told me that she was bullied periodically at work by some of the men because she always wore her boots. As he said, "You would only do that once to Jul because you would well be put in your place." But the main thing was that her beloved Joey didn't seem to mind how she looked or what anyone else thought about her. They were obviously a pretty solid couple, and both lived to a ripe old age with their birds and their boots.

Another local citizen who walked among us was a one-of-a-kind man whom we'll call Granville. If you grew up in my neck of the woods and happen to be sixty years of age or older, you'll know who this story is about.

Now this guy was an industrious individual who saved his money like no other. Silver dollars were a common currency then, along with fifty-cent pieces. When it came to coins, Granville didn't fool around. Coincidentally, he also owned and operated a sawmill.

One day in that mill, upon being paid for a job, Granville dropped a coin. Well, what a fiasco! All operations ceased; the saw was shut down, and conversations abruptly stopped. Granville declared, loudly and clearly, along with a few choice words, that no one could move until that coin was found.

Imagine a scene where you're emphatically told that you are not permitted to leave, whether you worked there with him or not. It didn't matter to Granville if you had a busy day ahead—there was a coin at stake. Now, here was a man who could never be suspected of having an inferiority complex, although "inferior" is how most people regarded him. So, the sawdust floors were swept, and every square inch was searched, but unfortunately for him, it was to no avail.

It was always difficult to determine, I remember, whether this poor, cantankerous fellow was upset or not because his face was a permanent, surly scowl on a good day. But on this particular day, he was extremely disgruntled. Surprisingly, he didn't attempt to frisk anyone for fear of the consequences, so the matter was dropped. Little did he know that Michael, the resident who actually relayed this story to me, and who normally got his logs cut at this particular sawmill, had actually seen the money drop. Michael said that as he bent over to pick up some of his cut lumber, he heard and saw a coin drop to the floor by his foot. He quickly pocketed it without anyone noticing.

Michael told me that he had often felt cheated by Granville on previous transactions and felt that getting the coin that had practically dropped in his lap was just meant to be. He smiled as he told me that he experienced zero guilt about keeping it. The man who was involved in the transaction where the coin was dropped told Granville that the money was somewhere in the mill, and he wouldn't be paying twice.

A relative of mine told me the same story a while ago as we reminisced about what a scourge that old man was. He also said that Michael told him that retrieving a single coin from the cooked old sod felt more like getting a twenty-dollar bill. Today, they would likely refer to that incident as karma.

My own mother told me an incredible story about the outlandish and cruel lengths to which this Granville would go in order to protect his money. He was also known for counting his money in the privacy of his kerosene, lamp-lit kitchen. That sounds quite normal, doesn't it? However, to take it one step further, he placed all the money in used tin cans. When one can was full, he would, under the cover of darkness, secretly bury it in the backyard. The only problem was that being as covetous as he was, the full cans multiplied quickly, and in due course, he literally owned a gold mine—by the standard of that day. That doesn't seem like much of a problem to have cans full of money, but by the time he was an old man, he forgot exactly where some of the cans had been placed.

He dug several holes out in his yard one evening, but there wasn't a can in sight. Becoming aggravated, and ultimately enraged, by this turn of events, he accused his poor wife, Aggie, of actually digging them up and stealing them. I remember poor Aggie. She was a short, tiny woman who was very soft-spoken, and I'm assuming that she was totally controlled by the ogre she had the misfortune to marry.

As Mom told it with great disgust, Granville placed a chair under an open rafter in the kitchen and demanded that she stand on it. Being totally intimidated by him, she did as he bid. Then the miserly monster proceeded to loop one end of a rope around a rafter and place the other end around her neck. With that, he yelled furiously, "Confess, old woman!" Aggie related to Mom that she was weak and trembling all over with fright but pleaded her innocence. Finally, as her husband tired of his tantrum, he loosened the noose and allowed her to step down. I guess that after living with this nuisance for so long, she was just happy that he hadn't actually hung her. Granville didn't put too much stock in the marriage vow to "love and cherish."

Now, there was a man who knew the meaning of a dollar. I think those dollars were the only friends he ever had. As a child, I only went near him if absolutely necessary. He was, for the most part, detested in Paradise. Other than operating his sawmill, he probably never had company of any kind.

Unfortunately for Aggie, he knew absolutely nothing about fairness, compassion, or sanity. Those money cans are probably still there buried in his backyard, but if they are, Granville didn't die happy. Probably a decent-living person eventually retrieved them, and if so, karma struck again in this old miser's life. He and his wife were childless so at least those unkind traits weren't passed on.

On the much kinder side was a resident by the name of Aunt Marion Lynch. That was her actual name, and one I'm proud to mention in this book. Aunt Marion wasn't my biological relative, of course, but as a child, who knew? She was a lovely woman who was thought to possess a God-given gift. She was Paradise's Charmer. That term certainly sounds a great deal more endearing than "witch-doctor," but basically, it was the same concept.

She stood approximately five feet four inches and always seemed to me to be very elderly, probably because she was so bent over in her stature. She always dressed in long black dresses and an apron. Her hair was white and pulled back in a tight bun, and she was one of the sweetest people God ever created.

In a fair number of houses at the time, there would often be what was called a "back kitchen." It was in this back kitchen that milk from your cows would be brought to a boil and pasteurized. "Pasteurized" wasn't the word we used, but that's what most people endeavoured to do. We knew that the milk had to be boiled to make it safe for drinking. It was then separated from the cream sitting on top. If you haven't tasted the cream that boils to the top of milk, then you haven't tasted cream. It was delicious and superior to any candy out there. I can't imagine what hefty price the supermarkets would charge for that delicious product now.

Mom would often send us down to Aunt Marion's for cream or milk. There she would quite often be in her back kitchen, dressed in her long apron, stirring the milk. She wouldn't hear tell of money exchanging hands. If Aunt Marion liked you or knew you were in need, she would scoop it up out of the pot with a ladle, pour it in a jar or bottle and pass it over with just a kind warning to be careful with it on your way back up the gravel road to your house.

Aunt Marion Lynch could easily have hung out a medical shingle over her door for all the knowledge she seemed to possess. But regardless of a shingle, medical diploma or not, the whole community knew exactly where to go when life presented them with a medical problem. It was a common sight to see someone you knew who was in ill health making their way to her door.

I was always fascinated and awestricken really whenever I visited her with a sick sibling or friend because it would appear to us that she could fix anything and have you right as rain in no time. She could adequately cure anything from a toothache, hives, warts, painful sties, and any kind of hideous infection. These were her specialties, and her services were in constant demand.

Thinking about Aunt Marion transports me sixty-odd years ago, right in the middle of her warm kitchen. My friend, Tommy Sharpe, had a terrible toothache, which earned him a couple of days home from school. But his toothache just seemed to keep on throbbing. So, off he was sent, with me in tow, to see what Aunt Marion could do to alleviate the problem. There we were, sitting on her kitchen chairs, with Tommy poking his fingers in his mouth while trying to tell her his troubles.

First, Aunt Marion would chew up a piece of tobacco and place it in on the infected area. Even if that infected area was inside your mouth, in went the chewed-up tobacco, along with Aunt Marion's saliva. Its purpose was probably to lessen the pain.

I remember being so intrigued by what was going to happen next. I can see her perfectly as she took off her wedding band and slowly made the sign of the cross over Tommy's cheek. She repeated that action three or four times as she mumbled a few phrases. It could have been the Lord's Prayer, but when you're eight years old, you imagined her mumblings to be some wondrous, magical incantation. Whatever it was, you could be assured that if Aunt Marion laid her hand to you, you were cured.

I don't know if it was all psychological or not, but on the way home, Tommy excitedly told me that the unbearable pain in his cheek left him as she was blessing and mumbling. We were both wide-eyed and dumb struck. I remember being unsure whether we should be scared out of our wits or thoroughly delighted. I'm pretty sure that Tommy wanted desperately to wrap his arms around her and give her a big kiss for ridding him of the awful pain. The other part of both of us just wanted to slowly and timidly back out the kitchen door and make a dash for home. It was incredible to witness. You really felt as if you were in the presence of something heavenly. And even if Aunt Marion couldn't perform medical miracles, she definitely was an angel and was loved by everyone in the vicinity.

I left Tommy at the bottom of his lane, ran all the way home, burst into our kitchen, and proceeded to inform everyone within earshot that my friend's pain was miraculously gone. Mom didn't seem to be the least bit surprised as she stood at the stove preparing our supper. She had all the faith in the world in the powers this miraculous lady possessed and spoke of her often in her later years.

It was about a year or two later that the same thing happened to me, and Mom sent me down to visit this lady for the same procedure. I remember that I had been in misery for days. Aunt Marion did exactly the same thing that she had done with Tommy, and I was flabbergasted when the pain left my tooth.

We'll never know about Aunt Marion and the nature of her healing gift, but she was indeed considered a miracle worker to those who believed in her powers, as I certainly did after my own encounters. I still prefer to think that she possessed magical powers. And to her credit, whatever her gift was, she always used it to the benefit of anyone who sought her assistance.

Tragically, her protective powers didn't include herself, because she experienced the worst form of pain for a mother. Her son, Jake, entered World War II, survived combat without a scratch, and happily came home to Paradise at the end of the conflict. But shortly after his return in the summer, he went swimming in Octagon Pond. He was known to be athletic and dove in with the intention of crossing the pond, as he had done numerous times before. It was considered a bit of a dare to do that, but many swimmers took it on without incident.

An uncle of mine witnessed that horrible accident and told me about it. It was very warm but overcast that day, he said, and a lightning storm came up quickly as Jake was halfway across the pond. As soon as the lightning was seen, everyone scampered out of the water to the shore. People were yelling to Jake to hurry and get across because of the lightning, but no one thought that the worst would happen.

It was said that he was too far out to quickly get out of the water and was struck by another flash of lightning. He disappeared beneath the water as many people looked on, horrified. His body was never recovered. That was a very sad day in Paradise, and especially in Aunt Marion's house.

Her second son, whose name escapes me, was walking home one night on Topsail Road; this was something he had done hundreds of times before. Just as he was about to make the turn to climb Flint Hill on the last lap of his journey, he was struck by a car and, unfortunately, was killed instantly. Traffic was never too heavy in those days, but he was still fatally wounded. The news that Aunt Marion's second son was killed spread quickly, and the horrible shock of it was felt through all of Paradise.

Her third son, Clarence, very often entered the door of our house and had many a cup of tea as he spoke to my parents. Mom would often remark that she really enjoyed his company, and he was very knowledgeable on most matters. He was a well-spoken and a quiet man, and everyone would comment on how fashionably dressed he was wherever he went. Clarence worked with Newfoundland Light and Power, and I'm sad to say that he was electrocuted on the job when he was in his mid-thirties.

Aunt Marion's three sons were all gone before their time. I don't know if that poor lady had a cure for a broken heart or if she could administer it to herself, but she would surely need it to cope with that much grief. She relieved so many people of their various ills and pains, yet her own life was filled with sadness in her older years. In her grief, however, she continued to administer her power over pain for anyone who came to her with an ailment. She never turned anyone away.

On to a more (and much-needed) light-hearted side, there was Josie. Now, poor old Josie was probably well into her sixties when I was a child. She was a married, pleasant enough woman, but she definitely wasn't very worldly. To tell the truth, I don't know if the poor woman even got as far as St. John's in the whole of her days. But I think it would be fair to say that she always appeared to be a little short-changed in her reasoning abilities.

Even though it certainly didn't put Josie in a very positive light, her husband often regaled locals with tales of his wife and her poor judgment. As a farmer, he was obligated to get to town with his horse and cart to sell his vegetables. Why he never took his wife on any of those trips to town, I don't know, because it would have been a real tonic for the deprived woman. Her husband had another horse, however, which he asked her to be responsible for in his absence on this particular day.

Merrily and alone, he went on his way to St. John's to sell his wares and left strict instructions for Josie to feed and water this horse sometime through the day. Toward evening, her husband got back home, and he inquired as to whether or not she had fed the horse. "Yes," replied Josie, "she had lots to eat but she wouldn't drink a thing. The glass is still out there with the water in it!" Apparently, she hadn't spent adequate time in any barn observing horses either. Either way, the poor lady was never quite on top of her game.

One day, over a cup of tea at our house, she asked my mother, "Florie, do you think there's more people in the world besides Paradise?" Now, that's what you call being secluded.

The poor unfortunate lady didn't have it easy in most ways. It was also a given in the area that once the vegetables and wares were sold in town, Josie's husband would arrive home on the flat of his back in the back of the cart, too drunk to steer. But, as it happened, he didn't have to steer anyway, thanks to their sensible horse. That smart animal knew his way by heart and always faithfully transported his master from a tavern on Water Street to his house in Paradise, which is not an insignificant distance.

Anyone who lived in Paradise was well used to observing the horse making its way over the hill and up our road all on his own. It would look like the cart was missing a driver until you saw the outstretched, unconscious creature in the back. Most residents would always wonder, as my mother did, when they watched the old horse slowly trudge along, whether any of the profits from the day's sales had made it home. Incredibly, the horse would neigh loudly when he arrived home, as if he was honking the horn to let everyone inside the house know that they were finally home. Then the man of the house would be carried in, as he would be too drunk to stand. It's really sad that Josie didn't know her way to town or anywhere that might offer her better living conditions than those she endured.

From harmless to horrible, we move on to our very own local witch. Now, as children, we wholeheartedly believed that this cantankerous, scary-looking, older female was the devil herself.. No "Aunt" here because no one ever wanted to get close enough to this old woman to call her Aunt. She was just Mabel.

As kids, we would stare at her from a distance because she had a striking resemblance to the witches we saw in books. To embellish that image, she used to make her own birch brooms from the woods.

We would watch her when she had them in her hands, expecting her to hop on and take to the skies at any second. You would often see her on the tarred roof of her little one-storey house with that birch broom, sweeping it off, or maybe trying to keep it clear of flankers (sparks). She was quite an elderly woman at that time as well. Whatever the reason was, she definitely fit the bill of a wicked and downright spooky witch.

It's safe to say that all of us were petrified of Mabel. We would certainly give her a wide berth as we quickly walked past her house because we secretly feared she would cast a spell on us. She would yell and shake her fists at you for just walking by her house, even if we had no intention of getting too close. There was always some kid who claimed to know for sure that she could make you disappear with a spell because, as they claimed, "She's done it before." Well, none of us needed to hear much more than that to stay well away from her premises.

She lived in a tiny, high-peaked roof house which, against all expectations, was surrounded by a gorgeous, colourful flower garden. Mabel spent a fair amount of time outside her house toiling over and nurturing her plants, so it wasn't always easy to get past her without being seen. I remember finding it strange that such a mean creature could have such a keen interest in anything as pretty as her garden. Maybe her family had a nice garden when she grew up in Salem!

All jokes aside, I'm sure the poor wretched soul was no witch. But she closely resembled one when she dressed in her usual, drab, black clothes, which were draped around her skinny body. Her skirts went to the ground, and her grey hair was pulled tightly back in a bun.

Most of the population lived right on the main road, so it was next to impossible not to encounter her when you passed by. Lots of times myself and my buddies managed to make it by her house without being detected but there were other scary times we would just get in front of her house and she would make an absolute mad dash to her fence. I can see her now, practically frothing at the mouth as she grabbed a paling of her fence. Then she would furiously wave that actual real homemade birch broom at us and she would yell the same thing every time to the top of her lungs "stay clear." And believe me, no one wanted to go anywhere near her.

In my child-like imagination, I was sure that she had to have a big, black cauldron sitting in the middle of her kitchen, bubbling and steaming away while she stirred whatever was in there with a four-foot spoon. That old woman was as intimidating as it got. All she was missing was the wart at the end of her nose and a tall pointed black hat.

While walking down Paradise Road, and without even mentioning her, we would instinctively cross over to the other side of the road once we got within thirty feet of her house. It was a habit for all the young ones in the neighbourhood as we walked up and down Paradise Road. We had conditioned ourselves to stay away.

But you know, in retrospect, the poor woman probably thought that fear was her only option to keep us away from her flowers. She didn't know that we had been taught a little better than that and would never have bothered her lovely flower garden. I will say, though, that it's good she wasn't growing chestnuts or rhubarb, which we loved. I'm convinced that she must have recognized our intense fear and our desire to get past her. Why she was so verbally abusive remains a mystery.

When my brave brother, Nelson, or Nels, as we always called him, was about twelve years of age, he once ventured in her backyard when she was nowhere in sight to take some dogberries hanging from her tree. Like a flash of lightning, out she swooped with black skirts flapping. Armed with a salt gun, she aimed and fired at him. To think she shot at Nels for sour, old dogberries, rather than sweet carrots or even her prize flowers is hard to fathom. Luckily for Nels, her aim was poor, and she didn't hit him, but he certainly didn't hang around waiting for the second shot. Can you imagine being that miserable? There were dogberries, come to think of it, on dozens of trees around our area, but I guess trying to confiscate anything at all from the "witch's" yard presented more of an exciting challenge to Nels.

Mabel really wasn't your stereotypical picture of a cookie-baking, hugging grandmother. She kept her hair in a tight bun and wore an apron, and that's where the similarity ends. She did, to our surprise, have nine grown children and numerous grandchildren, so she must have had a somewhat normal life, and even a husband, at some period during her time on this planet. Now you would understand if *that* man came home dead drunk at all hours in a cart pulled by the horse!

Older residents of Paradise would eagerly tell of a time during the Depression and the WWII years when a younger, but not happier, Mabel owned a small convenience store, which was actually attached to her house. Her reputation then, as a younger woman, was pretty much identical to the behaviour that I witnessed when she was much older.

The store she owned and managed sold items that had to be cut, measured, or weighed, such as butter, sugar, and flour, and plugs of Beaver tobacco. For the younger reader, plugs of tobacco somewhat resembled an Eatmore bar, but it was about four inches long and about two or three inches wide, and the aroma of Beaver tobacco was like a little piece of Heaven. Even those of you who weren't pipe smokers can remember, I'm sure, that a lit pipe filled with a cut of Beaver tobacco permeated the air like the world's finest perfume. Its smell was comparable to what a finely made chocolate would be to your taste buds. If it was around today, I think I'd take up a pipe. How cigarettes ever replaced it is mind-boggling.

Unfortunately for the consumer in Mabel's little store, her half pounds of butter and quarter plugs of tobacco were consistently smaller in size and higher in price. Such was her reputation. As a matter of fact, some supermarkets today use the same practice for the most part, and it's totally legal. Mabel was one of the first entrepreneurs in Paradise, and it seems like she got the ball rolling for the crafty, bigger businessman.

We didn't often patronize her store because you actually didn't get your money's worth, and also because Mom would have a job on her hands to convince one of us to go anywhere near there. I remember that when we had no other choice but to go on an errand there, we made sure that there were at least two or three of us, just for safety's sake. We constantly and nervously looked for that cauldron, and we wanted some support in case we had to fight her off. Oh, the imagination of youth!

Another couple of names of colourful characters that pop to mind are Bill and Ben Murphy. They were two harmless old souls who always lived together as bachelor brothers and were in their mid-fifties when I was young. Now, Bill, unfortunately, had serious sight problems and always wore very thick glasses. Observing him out in his garden tending to his vegetable patch, I would say that he was legally blind.

Ben, on the other hand, couldn't speak for some reason but just mumbled. Bill, curiously enough, seemed to understand whatever Ben tried to say, but we never could.

On one occasion, as a seemingly harmless prank, a group of boys visited Bill and Ben, as we all often did. We all liked the brothers, but I guess their ailments were just a little too tempting to a bunch of energetic boys.

My brother, Herb, and his friends, Ken, Dawson, and Hubert were all local and lived on our road. Those four boys specifically paid friendly visits to Bill and Ben through the year, without mishap, and did them a turn or two on occasion. This particular evening, as they made their entry into their house, they found that Ben was in the kitchen. As he couldn't speak, he pointed to the upstairs portion of the house and indicated to the lads that Bill had already gone to bed.

Herb told me that one of the boys had been helping his father tar their roof that day. Off they went to his house to get the bucket of remaining tar and a ladder. They rushed back to climb up to Bill's bedroom window. There, they proceeded to tar the window, waited for it to dry a little, and did their best to scratch out what roughly resembled a couple of stars on the window. It was all meant to be a bit of a lark. The boys nearly keeled over with laughter.

Whether it's true or not, the boys swore that Bill, with his poor eyesight, stayed upstairs in bed for two days, thinking it was night-time. I guess he was very well rested, but also very hungry when he finally got up. Of course, the group of them denied having done it when they were confronted. And the Murphy brothers obviously didn't hold it against them because the boys were still allowed in the house after that. I would say that the brothers made sure there weren't any ladders left lying around after that, though.

Bill and Ben Murphy's house. The women are unidentified.

Years prior to that, sometime during the 1930s, when Mrs. Murphy was still alive and Bill and Ben were much younger, her husband was working on Bell Island in the iron ore mines and would board over there during his employment. Cash was a rare commodity then, and Mrs. Murphy always conducted her business with coins. When Mr. Murphy would get paid, he would send money home to his wife. The truth be known, she had no idea what this paper was when she regularly received it in the mail.

A nephew of hers, who was a friend of mine, told me that he visited his aunt one day. Mrs. Murphy was telling him about this pretty paper his uncle had sent her from Bell Island. She brought him in the living room. And lo and behold, there was all the cash neatly glued individually to the walls. She thought the pictures on it were very attractive and decided to wallpaper with them, and he didn't have the heart to tell her the difference. True story!

She was just unfamiliar with currency like that and, of course, wouldn't waste it. She simply liked it. Her son, Bill, was unable to see what she had done in the front room, and Ben couldn't tell her. It's also not outside the realm of possibility that the boys weren't familiar with cash either, as most purchases in and around our area were done with silver dollars, fifty-cent pieces, and other coins.

They all survived through it all, and all the residents around, including the young culprits I mentioned, often helped that family with whatever needed to be done. The brothers cohabited, apparently quite happily together, and lived right into their eighties.

At this point, I absolutely have to mention a very fond memory from my childhood: Andrew Clark. Now, Andrew was one of Dad's closest friends and was always one of the men who would go to the Nickel Theatre, at the top of Garrison Hill in St. John's, to see a movie with Dad. Curiously, for some reason, it was only the men who went to the movies together, and the women went separately as well. Once married, that's one thing couples didn't do together. It didn't seem unusual at the time because that's all we knew. Looking back, however, it does.

Andrew was a welcome face at our table, be it for a game of cards or just a cup of tea and a chat with Dad.

This quiet fellow was never married and lived the whole of his life with his brother and his wife. He worked daily at landscaping, farming, cutting logs, and whatever else added up to a decent week's wage.

I remember that he always had a brand-new car, and his 1955 Chev was a beauty. He would let me drive it back and forth on our lane but would always warn me not to take it on the road. I suppose that he would warn me, given the fact that I was only about ten years old at the time.

Andrew was fond of a "drop" but never drank at the house because Dad never drank. Sometimes, he'd arrive at the house while wending his way home, always on foot, after a few social drinks somewhere. Mom would give him a bowl of soup or whatever she had to offer at the time. He never took a chance on hurting his car, himself, or anyone else when he planned on a night out.

If it was stormy and he was obviously not quite able to navigate on foot, he would say, "I'll wait 'till she dies down a bit," and then he would proceed to sit down by the side of the stove. Of course, the next thing, he was fast asleep. As kids, we would sometimes think that he was dead there in the corner of the stove as we watched, motionless, waiting for the next big snort and a mumble or two. When we were satisfied that we didn't have a dead man on our kitchen floor, we went to bed.

There was the odd occasion when he arrived in the same happy state and one of my parents would say, "Andrew, you can't go back out in that dirty weather, stay the night." Well, with the brood of youngsters in our house, there were no spare bedrooms. So, Andrew would slowly take off his coat and shoes and climb in next to Dad and Mom in their bed! He would be out cold in two minutes, and my parents made the best of it for the night. I think they both felt responsible for Andrew in a way because he had no wife or children, and he was more like a brother to Dad than anything. And Mom wouldn't see him in jeopardy for a fortune.

I'm sure that this story would hold sexual connotations today, but with poor old Andrew, it was just "keeping an eye out" for his welfare. He and my parents were friends until death, and he was a fine person.

So ends the characters of my childhood. I remember them, except for one or two scoundrels, with a real fondness. One thing you can say about Paradise: at no point was it ever a boring place to live. There was always someone who wanted to tell you a story and someone else making one of their own. Periodically, there was a new baby born who looked like another woman's husband, but that made for a hushed bit of chat over the clothesline. Nothing would be done about it regardless, as couples always stuck together. Assuredly, we had our own version of a soap opera at times, as most places can boast. How boring it might have been had we been perfect.

Yes, everyone pretty much knew everyone else's business, and at times that was really annoying and led to the odd dispute among neighbours. But overall, I think it actually made us closer.

Midwives And
Doctoring

It's only fitting that I initially pay tribute to Mrs. Dover, one indispensable woman in our hometown. To us, she was only known as "Mrs.," and as children, we never gave much thought that this lady might have a first name. Mrs. Drover was the unofficial midwife for Paradise, and she birthed all the babies, as far as we know, right through the 1930s and 1940s. She delivered both my older brothers, Herb and Lock, in our house. Babies were usually born right at home then.

Mrs. Drover had a lengthy career as a well-respected and knowledgeable midwife. Her expertise in delivering children was trusted, and she successfully saw a significant number of anxious mothers through their labour. Following that, she would visit them for days after the birth to monitor how the moms were doing with their new addition.

The doctor whom our mother visited during her pregnancy, for whatever reason, requested that she give birth to me, the third child, at the Grace General. After I was born in 1946, all my other siblings were born at the Grace as well, except for my twin sisters, Jane and Janet, who were two of the younger siblings.

On the day of their birth, the first twin surprisingly made her appearance into this world in the back of Dad's old 1952 Studebaker. A neighbour of ours, Lisa Sharpe, who was casually visiting our house when Mom went into labour, jumped in the car with Mom lying in the back seat and Dad nervously driving to the Grace Hospital, which was about eight kilometres away. Just as they drove down over Flint Hill, Mom said that she knew she wouldn't make it to the hospital. As Dad drove by Soper's Store, just a short distance from our house, the first baby arrived. Dad decided to pull into the Infectious Diseases Sanatorium on Topsail Road (known to locals as 'the San') to request help, and it was there that the other little twin was born.

As with all their children, except for my poor little brother, Melvin, who died as a baby, the twins were healthy, robust, and none the worse for wear. As Mom said later, the other thing that didn't go right that day was that since it was June, she had worn her brand-new summer coat, and it was ruined. But, as she calmly stated when all was said and done, "that wasn't too high a price to pay though for giving birth to not one, but two healthy babies while you were on the run." It was a real nail-biter for our Dad, though, and he was really relieved when the three of them finally got situated and examined at the Grace Hospital.

I have already mentioned a lady we fondly called Aunt Marion, our own sweet Charmer. As giving and attentive as she was, however, she wasn't by any means made responsible for all the nursing and healing of residents. The reason for that was that most adults were well versed in the methods of basic first aid and home remedies. These remedies always seemed to relieve sicknesses or injuries, but I don't know if they would be medically approved by today's standards. As a matter of fact, I would place a good bet that the first remedy I'm going to mention would never make it to a modern pharmacy.

My grandchildren are quite horrified and shake their heads in disbelief when I tell them that kerosene was one of those popular oral remedies. It was taken in a small dose, of course, but we still swallowed it! Yes, if you had a bad cold, the flu, or certainly a croupy cough, you were given a tablespoon of kerosene mixed with molasses—undoubtedly to kill the taste of the kerosene. It was a well-known and well-used "cure." I feel certain in stating that it was considered the perfect medication all over Newfoundland.

Then there was Minard's Liniment. No, not to rub on your muscles, for which it was designed, but again, to be mixed with molasses and poured down the hatch. Some of the older crowd used to drink it straight. Both cures were met with many a grimaced face when you finally managed to convince yourself to swallow it down.

Some younger people may think that I can't possibly be telling the truth, but it's an actual fact. I had to take it, and I'm sure many of you older folks can confirm that yes, indeed, kerosene and Minard's Liniment were taken orally.

It was my wife, a born and bred townie, who reminded me about the Minard's Liniment and molasses concoction because she was a victim of that herself. It didn't kill us, but maybe the thought of having to take it the second time was a good reason to get better. And to think everyone over eighteen smoked then! It's a wonder there weren't a few combustible deaths while administering that lovely concoction.

Can any of you remember—or I should say feel—the ever-reliable bread poultice? It makes me laugh to think about wearing those even though they always seemed to be productive. If there was an infection of any kind, maybe a boil or a whitlow, which was an infected and swollen area, usually surrounding a fingernail, you were subjected to a homemade poultice. Does anyone even get whitlows anymore?

Poultices were created with meticulous care and precision. Firstly, the parent who administered it would take a couple of crusts of bread or part of the heel of the loaf. I'm assuming that they did this for the drawing purposes of the yeast. Next, they wet the bread a little with boiled water, maybe to activate the yeast, shaved off a tablespoon or so of Sunlight Soap, maybe for its cleansing properties, and placed it onto the dampened bread. This concoction was put on a piece of clean cloth or bandage, applied directly to the affected area, and left for a day or two. It felt like what it was—a mushy mess—but miraculously, it worked beautifully, and your skin was never cleaner than it was after sitting in the Sunlight Soap for a couple of days.

Those poultices were, thinking back, one of the kinder remedies of the day in that they didn't hurt at all, and you smelled like freshly baked bread while you wore it!

It is time to pay homage to all the old-timers who knew exactly how to take control of a situation when accidents happened. That was simply because, I guess, they had seen it all or experienced it through their years. There was an Emergency Department that one could visit, but that always seemed far-fetched if you weren't dying. It would be the last consideration.

From the time I can remember, I used to love to accompany my Grandfather Rixon anywhere he went. It wasn't too often that he managed to go into the woods to cut some logs without having me tagging behind him. I would do whatever he asked me to do, and he would patiently explain the whys and wherefores as we did our work. What was even better was that he would tell me stories about when he was growing up as we went along.

One particular day is still vivid in my memory. I was about seven or eight years old, and I eagerly traipsed behind him into the woods behind his house. I happily pulled along a little cart that Grandfather had made just for me to gather wood. After about half an hour of vigorous chopping, I forgot Grandfather Rixon's number one rule when you have an axe in your hand, and I looked away. I missed the log. The axe slammed down right on my left hand, and I gave myself a substantial gash of about two inches in width.

The blood flowed freely because I was overheated from all the swinging of the axe. The very sight of it pouring out was so frightening to me, especially being that young, and in a minute, my coat and pants were red with blood. Quick as a wink, my grandfather cut some frankum (gum) off one of the trees, wiped away the excess blood to determine the exact site of the wound, and applied it directly to the wound on my hand. I had never seen him move that fast before in my life, which was scary in itself. Instantly, the flow of blood stopped, and I felt like I could breathe again.

Grandfather paid no more attention to the job we had been doing and very calmly explained that we had to go home now and come back for the wood and tools later. I know now that it had really scared him, but he didn't want to panic me. He made me sit in his homemade cart and pulled me out of the woods—so I wouldn't overheat any further, I think. By the time he got me to my kitchen door and my mother slowly removed the frankum with butter, the gash looked like it was starting to heal already. She cleaned it with some kind of solution, carefully wrapped it in a bandage, and apart from the throbbing in my hand, I felt nearly as good as new again. And when you're eight, proudly wearing a bandage is like having a first-place medal to show off.

I still have a visible scar from that experience, and it has always served as a lifelong reminder to have respect for anything that can injure you. More importantly, that scar is a loving memory of my Grandfather Rixon who acted quickly, took care of me, and checked on me daily until it healed. He was simply the best there was. I'm convinced that I could have been in a great deal more trouble that time, had it not been for his knowledge and fast action. I will be forever grateful.

If you were born anytime near the mid 1900s, you will remember the old-time medicine cabinets. You don't see too many of those today. It was about two and a half feet high and two feet wide, with a mirror on the front. It was always placed directly over the bathroom sink. There were only three or four glass shelves inside, and it was exactly that—a medicine cabinet. It wasn't a pretty item, but it was necessary, and every house had one. I can't imagine where we would have put all the hair and skin products most of us have now. And if you did have one, it usually included all the ingredients that you find in expensive over-the-counter medicines today. Remember the cure-all remedies we had, such as iodine and Mercurochrome? People were of the firm belief that if you had anything, from a hangnail to leprosy, you could put iodine on it and be as right as rain in no time.

As children, when we had a cut or skinned knee, we always prayed that our parents would select Mercurochrome to lather us up with because it looked the same but didn't have the awful sting of iodine. Both of these products came in a tiny glass brown bottle that was about three inches high with a little glass wand inside to apply the brownish, water-like liquid. And that brownish colour was like pure dye. I wonder if the women ever used a few drops of it on the roots of their hair back then.

Mercurochrome was taken off the market, apparently because it contained a small amount of mercury. Where were these people when we, as kids, had to slug back the kerosene? If you were treated with either one of these medicines, you could proudly display your battle scar in either varying shade of yellow, brown, or red. The more they applied, the darker you got, and it would stay on you until your next Saturday night bath!

Hives used to be a big problem back in the 1950's and 1960's. They were something like a boil—not as sore, but certainly very itchy. Where did hives go? You never hear tell of anyone suffering from them anymore. But when you did have them, you would be coated with a pink, chalky, substance that dried quickly and looked simply awful. It looked like you were covered in flour that wouldn't come off. It was called Calamine Lotion, and it is still on the market today. Since hives have disappeared, I don't know what it's used for, but thankfully, it was painless—awfully ugly but painless.

One Saturday night in September, just after having started Grade One, I sat in that beautiful, old tub we had in our kitchen, thoroughly embracing the comfort of the hot, sudsy water during our weekly wash. I had been sick for a week with a persistent cough that just wouldn't go away. I remember being taken out of the tub after a good scrub by my mother, dried off, dressed in the warm pyjamas that she used to hang by the woodstove, and then put in bed. You can well appreciate the sensation of warmth and comfort at any age.

Being clean as a new penny and so very comfortable in my warm pajamas, I immediately felt better. I battened down in bed with my brothers, ready for a good sleep. I definitely wasn't expecting to see my father appear in front of me with a big bowl of goose grease. Well, I wasn't sure what was going to happen next, but then I quickly recollected that the same thing had happened to my brother, Lock, a few months before.

My brothers moved away from me in the bed like lightening. Up came the pyjama top, and then Dad dipped his hands in the bowl, and I was smeared all over my upper torso with this goose grease; so much for the feeling of being clean and comfortable. I was so slippery that I'm sure I could've squeezed through the bedroom keyhole.

The old timers swore by goose grease to alleviate a cough or a bad flu. And let's face it, a large portion of the expensive remedies found on the pharmacy shelves today contain a lot of the same ingredients our ancestors used.

In my house growing up, our medicine cabinet continuously housed little vials of eucalyptus oil for children with croup, ginger wine for indigestion, lavender oil for infections such as eye sties and allergies, and, of course, goose grease was always kept on hand. The old people knew what was needed for different ills, whether it's ever been scientifically proven or not, and their faith in these was unshakeable.

Who of you can remember wincing as they were forced to swallow Brick's Tasteless (Castor Oil)? Tasteless, my foot! We would have to line up home in the kitchen, and one by one, with a screwed up face long before you even got to the "dreaded spoon" in anticipation of swallowing that stuff. Was there any so-called medicine out there with a viler taste than Brick's Tasteless, except perhaps the old, reliable cod liver oil?

Now, the fact that it came from a cod's liver, in my mind, didn't make it any more enticing, and being oil, it wouldn't have won any taste test either. But oil from a cod's liver was considered to be a magic potion for anything that ailed you. And, of course, we know today that it's still used and regarded as indispensable. Apparently, castor oil was good for your appetite, which makes me wonder why anyone in our house would even need it.

My hard-working parents had enough of a task to keep an adequate supply of food on the shelves as it was, with all of us as healthy and robust as we were. I guess they assumed that it was better to err on the side of caution and administer that horrible stuff on a regular basis.

As a youngster, I remember always being intrigued by these miniscule dark brown bottles in the medicine cabinet and taking them out for a look when no one was around to stop me. They were about one third the size of an iodine or Mercurochrome bottle. Some of these little, dainty bottles contained concentrated liquids containing ginger and spearmint for stomach problems. I remember being told that they were very "strong," which meant concentrated, I guess, and that just a small dose (half a teaspoon or so) of Ginger or Spearmint would be put in boiling hot water and drank. If that didn't work, out came the heavy-duty cure of baking soda (or "bread" soda), which was quickly thrown in a glass of water. Up it rose like a volcano in a cup, and I used to be horrified to see adults put that elixir to their lips and drink it down in a couple of gulps. It seemed wonderfully brave to me. That potion usually did the trick for the indigestion, and was the most popular remedy.

Eucalyptus oil, which impressed me even if you could pronounce it, was mostly used as a decongestant. A couple of drops in hot water were often placed near a baby's cot if they had croup, and it was also used for cold and flu. A pan of hot water, a little Eucalyptus oil, a towel to put over your head to catch the steam, and you were your own doctor.

It might appear that our shelves were not adequately stocked with what a current doctor may prescribe, yet Paradise residents lived healthy and long lives, for the most part. And most of the caregiving was done at home by parents. I personally had never been hospitalized, except for my birth, until I reached the age of sixty-three, and that was short-lived. I think that speaks well of the childhood health regime we went through, the old remedies, and also those who administered them.

No Child Labour
Laws Here!

There was never a time, I don't think, that I had to look for an activity to amuse myself as a child. As a matter of fact, you weren't always given an opportunity to amuse yourself because we all had to pull together as a family unit to sustain life as we knew it. By the age of six or seven, a youngster always had chores. And the frame of mind was not one of trying to avoid the work you were asked to do. We just accepted our jobs and got on with them. We never thought about *not* doing them mostly, because that wasn't an option anyway. It was as simple as that, and the cycle just merrily revolved from day to day.

As I mentioned earlier, a school day would often be started by gathering up your bundle of wood, quivering in your boots while rushing over to our schoolhouse, and lighting the potbelly stove. If you weren't lighting the fire in school, it could well be your turn at home to go out in the yard and bring in some firewood and splits. Those we had usually cut previously to get our own stove operating and pumping out some heat—and then some breakfast.

Parents didn't ask more than once back then because they didn't have to. It wasn't so much that we were afraid of the repercussions, because I don't think I ever heard my father raise his voice in the whole of my life. Mom was a great deal more outspoken than Dad and wasn't too slow in informing you if you weren't pulling your weight, but we all pitched in and shared the chores when time came to do them. It all worked like a well-oiled machine.

Quite often, our Uncle Jim Rixon would come to our house looking for some extra hands for cutting sods, usually when he would land a significant job from St. John's. Uncle Jim, who was Dad's half-brother, was much like Dad in manner and was just as hard a worker. His father-in-law was Cecil Lynch, and it was on Mr. Lynch's land in the middle of Paradise that we would cut all those sods.

I've tried my hand at various jobs in my lifetime, and cutting sods is certainly not work for a lazy man—or a lazy boy, which was all we were then. I can see us all now, manned with just an axe and a grubber. A grubber was essentially a pick on one side, and the other side flattened in order to uproot the sod. We grunted and groaned as we cut all of those sixteen-by-sixteen heavy sods and loaded them up in Uncle Jim's truck. Some of the new gyms that have sprouted up over the last few years should incorporate a sod cutting class into their workouts. The weight loss and muscle gain would be impressive, I'm sure.

A day before Uncle Jim planned on cutting those, we would enthusiastically jump aboard his dump truck, and off we'd go down to Miller's Path in Paradise, where we dug topsoil by hand until the truck was full. Thinking about it now, none of us ever had an extra pound on our bodies growing up, and for good reason. We were steadily working at some sort of manual labour, all in the purpose of helping some family member make a dollar, which was what life was all about.

Next would be a little expedition to the site in St. John's to offload the topsoil. That topsoil served the same purpose as underlay in carpeting, and it gave a good base for the sods. When all that was finally done and spread out, the shovels were thrown aboard the truck, and we made our way tiredly home. At this point, we knew that Uncle Jim would make a stop, take out his wallet, and buy us a couple of treats. They were simple pleasures but ones which we happily anticipated.

We were too young to articulate it, but we had great respect for the hard and never-ending labour that both of our parents regularly took responsibility for. But if, by chance, any of us happened to take too much time on a particular chore, an adult only had to speak sternly once, and we got the message and got going.

Mom used to laugh heartily as she reminisced about one of the more distasteful chores, to say the least, that she was obligated to perform when she was a child being raised on our road back in the 1930s. I feel compelled to add, as they say on TV, "Please be advised that the following story is not for the weak of stomach." In other words, as Newfoundlanders would say, if you're easily "turned," turn the page. Here we go with Florie's childhood story.

My grandfather, Billy Parsons, was a farmer and a butcher, and therefore obviously had to raise and kill his own livestock. When it was time for him to butcher a cow, all the blood was kept, so it could be mixed in puddings and sausages. The old folks told it like it was back then: he was preparing to make "blood puddings," and they are still called that today. I remember those puddings being the tastiest food ever, and I've never eaten any as good as my Grandfather's, except for Halliday's Butcher Shop on King's Road in downtown St. John's. That butcher shop has been around for a little over one hundred years, and the taste of their puddings brings me right back in time to when I delighted in having a meal of those prepared by Grandfather.

Periodically, a cow would be brought in the barn, and there, among the hay and all that was familiar to her, she would go to her eternal reward with a couple of hard knocks to the head. It was not a pleasant task for my grandfather, but it was a very necessary one. He knew that his family had to be fed and provided for. The carcass would be hoisted up via pulleys, and the neck would be cut so the animal could bleed out, and then it was paunched. While the animal bled out, the blood would be gathered in tall buckets. This blood would, of course, still be at their body temperature, which was too warm to let sit.

This is where the real fun started for my mother and her siblings. With hands washed and sleeves rolled up, they would have to kneel down to the buckets, put their bare arms in those buckets, and slowly stir the blood for about half an hour or an hour, while it sufficiently cooled. If they didn't constantly stir it, the blood would coagulate (that sounds much better than clot), and it would then be unusable.

Now *there's* a job you could only get a child or teenager to do, because no adult would want it. Sometimes it was emotional, if the cow was one that you were particularly fond of, but even as a child, my mother knew that it was necessary. If nothing positive could be said about that procedure, she had remarked, the blood was nice and warm on a colder day! How is that for eternal optimism springing forth from a little girl?

You may never again be able to look at a blood, or "black pudding" again in the supermarket. But the cow's blood is actually one of the main ingredients of those puddings we all know and love.

I used to regard the Italians' process of squashing grapes with their feet a little reprehensible until my mother shared that memory with me. And I would hazard a guess by saying that the young teens today doing an eight-hour shift at the McDonald outlets would feel somewhat comforted by their current job descriptions if they read the preceding pages.

Once all the roasts, sausages, puddings, steaks, etc. were cut, categorized, and made up for sale, Grandfather Parsons would, in my young memory, load up the homemade, wooden meat storage box, which was attached to his old 1946 Ford truck. Loaded up with all the usual vegetables that he grew in his vast fields, alongside eggs, berries, wood junks, splits, and his meat box full, off he would go to reap the profits of all the hard work done by himself and his family.

I can close my eyes now and see that old truck making its way down the dusty, unpaved Paradise Road on its way to St. John's and surrounding areas to sell his wares. All of that effort was just routine to him, and to us, actually, but recalling what it took to get the end product on that old Ford truck is downright inspiring.

The odd Saturday, he and my grandmother, Maggie Parsons, would leave at early morning, well stocked up for a long, unpaved journey to St. Mary's, where Grandfather had built up a significant clientele. They would often be invited to stay overnight by one of those loyal customers, so it was a little social outing as well. To add to that, they were outside of Paradise, with different faces and different scenery, and that was a rare commodity for either one of them. It would have indeed been a long day if they had to return in the evening.

What is now a leisurely, two-hour afternoon jaunt was then a weekend trip for my grandparents, and one they both looked forward to. If they came back with an empty truck, which they normally did, it was a win-win situation all round, with time well spent and money made. However, the truck wasn't always empty on the return trip home, because it was from the St. Mary's area that my grandfather usually bought the odd heifer or a few sheep. Going out there was a well-rounded business venture because everyone bought and sold.

While they were gone, Grandmother Parsons made it understood that, on their return, she was to be met with a spotless house. There was no such thing as throwing a party while the parents were away. Mom and her sister, Marg (Parsons) Hussey, worked diligently at scrubbing the floors and polishing anything that could be polished on those weekends. Their efforts had to meet the high expectations of their mother, or it would have to be done again.

Having said that, however, scrubbing and polishing probably seemed like a walk in the park to Mom and Aunt Marg, since these were the same young girls who had the chore of being up to their elbows in hot animal blood a few days before. All in one's perspective, I guess. In Paradise back in the day, "chillin' out" was not a well-known concept— or even an option—when there was work to be done.

Recently, my wife and I went back to Grandfather Parsons's fields to see if there were any remnants of his drills. His farm was situated on approximately fifteen acres of land overlooking Adam's Pond. And indeed, there is still evidence of his many drills for vegetables, which all his children and grandchildren worked on with him. How I wished that just once more, I could see him planting his crops with his faithful horse, Terry. I honestly don't know which one of them worked harder.

It was taken for granted that you would run down the road to help Grandfather weed all those crops in the summer. It was a back-breaking activity, even when you were ten years old. I can't imagine how he felt at sixty and seventy, bent over those rows and rows of carrot and potatoes, and every other plant that was feasible to grow in our climate.

Often, when we finished helping Grandfather weed his crops, we would go over to our friend Jack Lynch's house and help him weed his father's garden. After all that bending and pulling, Jack and the rest of us would often make a mad dash for Adams' Pond, where we would throw ourselves in the cool water. Nobody ever worried about swimming trunks for swimming. We were so overcome with the heat after working that we would strip down to our underwear and dive in. And if it was a particularly hot day, we all skinny-dipped. It felt so invigorating to go from weeding and sweating to yelling at the top of our lungs as we ran stark naked into that beautiful pond. It made the whole day's work worthwhile.

Billy Parsons was my mother's father, and he was a short, stout man whose daily uniform consisted of a long-sleeved shirt, which would be rolled up in the summer and rolled down in the winter, along with a pair of work overalls, one strap up, and one faithfully down! And on his feet would be his knee-high, black rubber boots, which he always referred to as his "goat rubbers." He was the picture of a farmer, and he certainly deserved our regard because he knew his stuff.

My maternal grandparents, Billy and Maggie Parsons. This picture was taken in our backyard in the mid-1960s on the day our twins, Jane and Janet were born.

Grandfather (which is what all his grandchildren always called him) also had to cut his hay once it reached a certain height. There were no combines anywhere near Paradise at that time, so he cut all that hay by himself using a scythe. If you're not familiar with them, scythes are shaped like a bow, with a long, single-edged blade, which are swung from left to right, parallel to the ground. Talk about your workouts. He would cut it and leave it to dry for a couple of weeks, and then it was our job to rake and bundle it.

We weren't allowed to go anywhere near that scythe because the blade had to be razor-sharp, but don't say we didn't want to. He would sharpen that scary-looking weapon with an oblong stone and do that so quickly that you would be frightened to watch in anticipation of him losing fingers while doing it. But miraculously, and thankfully, he never injured himself.

Once the hay was dried, he would put Terry, his faithful horse, to work transporting it to the barn. Now, I think Terry was Grandfather's best friend, and he loved his horse dearly. Terry worked alongside of him every day for many years, as he plowed the fields like a tractor does today. And every day, Grandfather would talk away to that old horse like it was a person and ask him questions, which he'd answer himself. I can hear him now quietly saying, "That's enough for a while, now, isn't it, Terry b'y? We'll take a little spell." Then he lovingly patted him down and gave the old horse a carrot, an apple, or a drink of water.

Grandfather Parsons' fields, where we all spent so much time helping him with his crops. That's Adams Pond in the background, where we often swam after a day of weeding.

L-R: Kelly Parsons, current co-owner of Grandfather Parsons' fields, and me.

When we were finished raking the hay, a box cart would be tackled up to Terry, and we would fill it. Give Terry a tiny tap on the hindquarter, or just say, "That's it, Terry," and that's all he needed. Off he would slowly trot to the barn and wait for us to follow him, where we unloaded the hay from his cart and stacked it in to feed the animals for the winter.

While hay was being pitchforked in, Grandfather would busy himself spreading coarse salt over each layer of hay to preserve it for the upcoming colder months. I learned so much from him as he went about his daily chores, explaining the reason for doing each task.

We would then pick up many of the seeds that had fallen off the hay and throw them in a brown bag in preparation of next year's hay crop. It was recycling, preservation, and education, all at its best from a kindly teacher.

Often in the fall of the year when the very last of his vegetables were harvested, Billy Parsons gave old Terry, the horse, a well-deserved day off, loaded up the truck with whatever was left, and took his grandsons to St. John's. That was a real treat in itself, because you didn't normally get anywhere other than within a mile radius of your own house on most days. We were excited to go just to take in the sights.

Once we arrived within the City limits, we knocked on as many household doors as it took to sell everything on board. People living in St. John's had no gardens and were usually happy to see us. When we were finally sold out, we would be awarded with fifty cents each, and back then, that was quite the prize. Keep in mind that it was probably 1955 or so. You could buy an armful of treats at Mrs. Gosse's store, maybe a package of caps to fire off, and still have change left. Oh, the choices!

Back on the farm, we always kept an eye out for the odd vegetable that hadn't grown well and was probably not fit for consumption or selling. Those would be put in the fodder pile, which Grandfather explained was kept as feed for the animals. There was the odd time, naturally, that myself and a few of the boys would spend some time trying to pitch and splatter a rotting potato off each other's clothes, but only when there were no adults around to discipline us. We were always out for a bit of frivolous fun wherever we could find it, but there was never a vegetable wasted that could be reused, and our Grandfather seemed to have a use for everything.

It was from this experienced gentleman that I learned about crop rotation. I would wonder, as a small boy, why one year he would reap a healthy crop of turnips in one field and then, instead of setting turnip again the next year there, he would set oats for hay. And where the potatoes grew abundantly one year, he would set turnip or carrot the next. He was, of course, rotating his crops so that the soil would not become depleted but remain mineral-rich. He would use terms like "harrowing the ground," which meant that there were no clumps in the soil, and the rows, called drills, looked even and uniform.

Annually, in the early Spring, he would treat the land with all the manure gathered from the animals over the winter, which was mixed with store-bought fertilizer. He had, more than likely, bought that at Gaze Seed Company. He was a popular patron there, as most farmers of the day were. When I was young, Gaze Seed was on Buchanan Street, off Water Street West in St. John's, and I think it was well established even then. That building was just very recently demolished, but Gaze Seed is still alive and well in another location in the downtown sector.

Then came one particular and unforgettable day when Grandfather Parsons gave Herb, Lock, and I a plot of land to set out our very own crops. We were just young boys! How energetically we tackled that small piece of land. In no time, we had the drills scooped out, the seeds in, the watering done, and we sat there watching for the first sprout to appear. With a little experience gained from assisting and observing Grandfather, the three plots eventually and proudly yielded about 45 sacks of potatoes for the family. Dad was obviously proud of his boys too because he built us a pound in the pantry about five feet tall, three feet wide, and three feet deep, which we filled to the brim. Without doubt, there was no shortage of mashed potatoes that Fall.

Caplin was a great fertilizer for crops, too, he told us. So, during the caplin skull in late May or early June, we would be treated to an excursion down to Horse Cove Beach to run like the wind into the salt water with our rubber boots on and scoop up enough caplin to cover the fields. We were always enthusiastic about catching these miniature fish, not so much due to the good fertilizer they provided, but because it was such fun to run out in the water with your net and get as many as you could. Many times, we fell in and were soaked in the salty water, but that was half the fun. And boys will be boys, even if we did get too many for our fields and intentionally filled our rubber boots with the sea water.

It was customary that you always brought home a 'feed of caplin' for supper, which Mom would promptly fry on the pan with lots of butter. Fried caplin and homemade bread was a fantastic meal, and our mouths watered as they all fried on the pan and we waited for supper to be called.

If I close my eyes, I can go directly and happily to Grandfather Parsons's fields, breathe the sweet-smelling, fresh air, and feel the hay all around me as I lay in it with my brothers or friends.

I'll never forget one sunny day up in the fields, when I just finished weeding the vegetables with my brother, Herb. We sat off on the bank, enjoying the sun, and Grandfather joined us for, as he would say, "a little spell" or "a little blow" while he'd drink a cool sip of water.

He would sometimes remark that he was finding his leg, which, as all Newfoundlanders know, meant that he was experiencing some pain there. As he rubbed it that day, trying to alleviate his discomfort as he sat between Herb and me, he casually explained that he was wounded during the First World War. We were speechless as we looked at each other, shocked but absolutely thrilled, and we pleaded with him to tell us the rest of the story.

Reluctantly, after stating that it was years ago, he informed us that when he was a mere eighteen or nineteen years of age, times were tough for him and a good many other people on the island, and employment was scarce. So, he decided that the best way out was to go away and find a job that would pay a decent wage. He had never strayed too far from home, but he really felt the urge to travel. He was young and willing to work while he saw the world and dreamed that hopefully, he would find a better situation for himself.

So, with what little clothes he had and a few dollars in his pocket, he told his family that he was off to find better work. That was true, of course; he just left out the part where he had planned to stow away on a ship bound for greener pastures. So, on his arrival to the waterfront in downtown St. John's, he milled around with the locals and longshoremen, looking for information.

He inquired as to what ships were going where and when and decided, then and there, that he was going on the first one leaving the island. That was quite a decision for a young man barely out of his teens. Once he found the exact time this freighter was going to disembark, he quickly made a few rounds on Water Street to gather up some much-needed items, such as food and drink, which he put in the brown bag he had brought from home. With just the clothes on his back and another "shift," which means a change of clothing in his bag along with a few jingles in his pocket, he carefully (and nervously, I would imagine) worked his way up the gangplank.

He stowed away behind a big dory and other equipment in a hidden corner and set off on this freighter, which was bound for England. I remember him saying that he got a little brazen after a few days and started to walk the decks with a mop in his hand. He stole some food and drink when he had the chance, and while eavesdropping on the workers going by his dory, he could determine how much longer he had to hide out.

Luckily for him, he was never detected, and he made it to shore in one piece without being thrown overboard. He said that he had speculated while lying awake at night, staring up at the stars, what they would do to a stowaway. He nervously concluded that he probably should have thought it through a little longer. That wouldn't be an experience for the faint of heart, nervously waiting to be discovered with the sound of every approaching footstep and voice.

Shortly after arriving in England and joyously disembarking the freighter without incident, he spent what little money he had left on food and board for a few days. Grandfather told us that he found room and board at the tallest stone house he had ever seen, and it was just off the waterfront. A few days later, having gotten his land legs back, he was determined to find the proper location where he could join the navy. He had made that life-changing decision while he watched all the sailors on the freighter.

He was relieved and happy when he passed the proper tests and met the qualifications to be eligible to enlist, and he did so right away. He couldn't believe his luck. Just after leaving home, he was on a payroll in another country. So far, his plan was working wonderfully, but there were to be tough times ahead.

After basic training for a few weeks and managing to sign his name on the dotted line, he donned the uniform and became a member of the British Royal Navy. He was proud to have found stable work, and more importantly, stable money, even though it was meager pay at the time.

Not long after joining up, World War I erupted. The first few months were uneventful and he had been at sea docking at various ports. Then, within a second, disaster struck ! He said that as often as you had heard about German U-Boats, while assigned to watch, you never saw signs of one coming up or even a periscope in the water as you scanned meticulously with binoculars.

This glorious, sunny day while Grandfather worked on deck, he suddenly felt as if the ship exploded. A torpedo from a U-boat hit them dead on while they were miles out at sea. In a flash, he found himself thrown into the salt water in intense pain from, he learned later, the several pieces of shrapnel that had pierced his leg. He didn't know if he was in shock, he told us, but he just tried to stay afloat and felt like he was having a really bad dream. It couldn't be real.

With his ship sinking before his eyes, Grandfather hung on to a piece of plank blown from his doomed ship, as did a few more of his shipmates who had managed to escape. He didn't know how serious his wound was but, at least, the pain from it kept him awake so he didn't slip under the waves. The continuous bobbing of the water as you hung on to a piece of plank was hypnotizing, he said.

As his leg was bleeding continuously, he was told later that it was a miracle to have survived at all, given that there were sharks and various other dangerous marine life in the waters. After three days of this misery, he said that dying didn't really seem like a bad idea. But thank goodness, on that third day, they were spotted by an allied ship and rescued. He thought that he was a goner but gratefully, the Lord had other plans for our Grandfather.

After being patched up by the ship's medic, he and his shipmates were transported to a hospital when they docked, where he underwent immediate surgery. Believe it or not, after the operation, the surgeons or nurses gave him that shrapnel in a little specimen bottle. He kept that bottle, and periodically, if we tormented him enough to retell that story, he would take out that odd-looking shrapnel for us to examine.

We were always proud of him anyway, but having your Grandfather stowaway on a ship, join the Navy, go to war, survive being adrift after being injured by Germans, and having the evidence to prove it made him seem like a real live hero to us. I don't think I ever looked at him in the same light again. He was a loveable old fellow anyway, but now he was the bravest loveable old fellow in my books.

How many times, at the end of an exhausting day, would that old sailor sit with us down in the field and tell a few yarns about his British Navy days during the war, the ships he worked on, and the wonderful places he visited. Listening attentively to his every word, I always thought that he already had a full life packed into the years he had spent growing up and serving in the Navy. However, he was less than twenty years of age when he returned from England.

My brothers and I would watch in delight as he showed us the mermaid that he had tattooed on his arm back in his Navy days. We would always torment him until he gave in and demonstrated. Whatever way he twisted that short, muscular arm, it looked as if that mermaid was actually dancing—quite a treat for a young boy! He also had a three-masted schooner tattooed right on the full of his chest, which looked pretty impressive to those of us who had never even seen a schooner with one mast!

I can't imagine a better setting for a child than those fields filled with various crops. We were out in the fresh air, under blue skies, and learning how to cultivate the land. Meanwhile, we listened to our Grandfather tell us stories of his youth and rode good old Terry the odd time when our work was complete. I witnessed many a breathtaking sunset over Adams' Pond and Grandfather's fields during those days, and I'm eternally grateful that I shared all of those precious hours with him and members of my family.

Visiting Royal's
Pond – Once A Year

If you think about it, before our houses and our culture became equipped with all things automatic, living was full of those little— and not-so-little—jobs needing to be done to maintain a regular and consistent existence. I can fondly recall not having any electricity and that meant cutting an adequate supply of wood for the stove for cooking and washing every solitary day. Wood was a staple we could not do without.

I find it amusing now, as an adult, when I see an old movie from the 1930s or 1940s and see electric ranges in the kitchens. In Paradise, we were aware of these appliances, but they didn't make their way up our hill, onto our road, and into our homes until the 1960s.

In my childhood, a hefty supply of wood for burning was needed seven days a week, summer and winter alike. Obviously, the bulk was needed in the winter for heat as well as cooking. I often watched my mother on the hot summer days, wiping her brow as she closed the woodstove door after putting six or eight pans of bread in to bake. Of course, she kept a watchful eye to each batch as it rose and browned in that lovely, old, and reliable stove.

Our family annually welcomed a new baby, and if Mom wasn't changing a diaper, she was making bread for her huge and hungry brood. But each delicious loaf and every pot of soup she worked so diligently to produce required wood in that old stove, and that task was undertaken each Fall down at a popular local spot known as Royal's Pond.

Royal's Pond is located right off main Paradise Road, down through what was known then as Miller's Path, which has since been renamed Camrose Drive. Looking at a current map of this area, as you travel further down Camrose Drive, it once again becomes Miller's Path. It was a good trek through the woods with horse and cart, but it was certainly a necessary one.

The whole male population of Paradise and the surrounding area, with a few exceptions, would prepare for the annual event by collecting every tool necessary to gather an ample winter's supply from the neighbouring woods. The shores of Royal's Pond were at capacity for a week or so while most male residents did their utmost to reach their quota of wood. At the time, it seemed as if every family in and around our little community was represented at this worthwhile venture, because obviously, we all needed heat, and that was the only option.

Box carts and slides would be tackled up to a horse or pulled manually, and down we would all trudge over the hill and a good distance into the thickly wooded area surrounding the pond. Every man and young boy made their way to a certain designated side of the pond. The men looked forward to the break in their regular routine of farming, tending to their mills, and all that went with rural life. It was hard work cutting and hauling that wood, but it was also an opportunity to talk and compare notes with all the other men living around us. It was a collaborative effort on everyone's part, and every family member was expected to (and usually did) pull their weight.

The path to Royal's Pond, where we annually cut our wood supply.

To all the wives and daughters, we must have looked like an army going off to war with all our paraphernalia. Mom generally followed us out the lane, making sure there were mitts and caps enough for the day ahead and constantly warning us, especially the younger and more inexperienced boys, to "keep an eye" on the axes.

It must have been a time-worn tradition, because each year, once we got to Royal's Pond, the same family would select the same spot. They would lay down their tools and bags, then gather wood to prepare a fire for later, when we would gladly suspend operations for the well-earned dinner break. We all knew who "owned" each area, and you respected that. The Pennell family worked the same piece of woods every year, as did the McCarthy and Rixon families, and so on right through each group.

Armed with handsaws, bucksaws, axes, and any other tool that would help yield a much-needed supply, we eagerly started in cutting. There was the odd conversation here and there, and people stopped to load up their pipes or have a chew of tobacco, but the pace was consistently busy. It usually took several trips to unload our sleds back at the house and several days to ensure that we all had enough cut. Each family kept vigorously chopping and loading until your father usually gave the word that you had met the required quota and the job was successfully finished. Grandfather Parsons always lent us old Terry on those expeditions, so that we didn't have to manually try to make that grade up from the pond. And old Terry never let us down.

Our old faithful horse, Terry, hauling the wood up an incline from Royal's Pond.

There were no chainsaws or skidoos with trailers to make the job a little less back-breaking back then. It was muscle, elbow grease, and sweat as each family energetically built their own pile. If you were within half a mile from Royal's Pond, you could quite easily hear all the axes striking the trees as most men toiled relentlessly to fell the trees, stack, and finally make the trek home with their wood.

As most normal communities can boast, there were a few lazy souls who always found an excuse not to pitch in or show up at the pond, but somehow, they managed to acquire wood, honestly or otherwise, from somewhere. You could nearly set your clock by these guys finding reasons for not joining in on those days, but they were worse off for it once the cold weather hit, and they missed a special time to my mind.

It didn't strike me way back then when I trotted down over that hill with my brothers, father, and grandfathers, but it was such a close bonding time for the men in each family. It wasn't every day that we worked together on the same project. It most certainly brings a smile to my face now to picture all that activity, and it would be a pretty sweet sound to my ears to hear all that chopping, the yelling back and forth, coaxing the horses with the heavy loads up over the hill, and our father finally acknowledging the job's end by saying, "all done, boys."

Cecil Lynch's garden with a woodpile from Royal's Pond, ready to be cut.

Even though the women never participated in the actual sawing and lugging down on Royal's Pond, their presence was unmistakable in the sizeable parcel of food that was carefully prepared and quickly eaten halfway through the day. After three or four hours of wielding an axe or saw, a fire would be lit on the side of the pond to make tea, and we would really look forward to your "dinner." The mid-day meal was always referred to as dinner, and not lunch, right up to the 1970s.

I used to look forward to the eventual smell of the wood burning from the hearth we had built earlier, because I knew that we would get to eat as soon as the water from the pond was boiled. So, there we would be, sitting on a stump or cross-legged on the shore, with a cup of hot tea in a mug from the old, blackened kettle or tin can. Then we were all free to avail of the sandwiches, teabuns, and cake stored in a box for the Pennell 'men' to share.

On reflection, I'm amazed and proud to think of how exception-ally well the majority of the families functioned as a community to provide all that much-needed wood supply. You can be sure too that no sedatives were ever needed for sleep those days.

Of course, it would have been far easier to adjust a thermostat like today, but that doesn't come with fantastic memories of an outing in the woods or a generous boil-up with friends and all the males in your family. It was a wonderful experience and I thank God for the memory of it.

The Long-Awaited
Christmas Season

We're living in a society where we still get that nostalgic Christmas feeling, and we still buy presents for the ones we love. That special feeling is usually brought on with the commencement of Christmas music from every radio station and media source, starting in early December for most of the population, and even a little earlier for other enthusiasts. Then we have some ambitious decorators, in homes and stores, getting that tree up and adorned not long after Remembrance Day is honored. Initially, I cynically believed that it was all done to get buyers out there earlier, armed with their credit cards. The earlier they buy, the more they buy in most cases. But on the other hand, and not so cynically, an early Yuletide Season also makes for a pretty multi-coloured environment and anticipation.

For me and many others my age, once you caught a glimpse of the bucket loads of paint coming in over your doorstep, that was the trumpeting in of the season. I'm sure you younger readers are quizzically saying, "What does he mean... paint?" Well, Christmas was synonymous with the prettying up, painting, and sometimes wallpapering of the inside of our house.

Where the tradition came from, I don't know, but in most Newfoundland homes, the thought of December 25 getting close meant that your walls would soon be a new colour as men whipped out their stir sticks and got to work. In the Pennell household, they didn't stop there. Every couple of years, at the same time, new rolls of canvas (locally referred to as "can-a-vas") showed up. Once the walls were all freshly painted with a coat or two, the new flooring was put down. It was like having a new kitchen and front room, even if you had to tolerate the overpowering smell.

As we all now realize, that paint that was being generously applied inside the house, and certainly in the front room, was oil paint. The smell would linger for the best part of a week, and we all inhaled those noxious fumes and thought nothing of it, except that we were happy that Christmas was on the way. Of course, who knew it was dangerous to do that? And if we had been told, we probably would have just shrugged it off. But dangerous or not, the smell of oil paint to this day is a great memory for me of all those Christmases I enjoyed up on Paradise Road. To me and many other youngsters, that pungent smell meant that Santa would soon be visiting our house.

Sometime during mid-December, Mom would always don her best coat and hat, and accompanied by three or four of us, she would venture to go to downtown St. John's. Since Dad was always working then, we had the overwhelming delight of being transported to what seemed to be a bustling metropolis by the United Bus Line, which stopped down at the bottom of Flint Hill on its way from Holyrood. All the bright, yellow buses that carefully made their way in from the various bays made their final stop on George Street in downtown St. John's, which was a calm, quiet, and business-like street back in the 1950s.

You have to realize that it was extremely exciting when you were seven or eight years old, coming from our one-road Paradise, to take in the sights on Water Street. It was like a miniature Las Vegas to us with all the streetlights, Christmas lights, traffic, and crowds of people with their packages. Holding on to Mom or one of your siblings' hands as you walked along, you would often hear a Christmas carol coming from one of the coves off Water Street. Invariably, it would be the Salvation Army Band, fully dressed in uniform, with their trumpets and tubas giving it their all while they tried to collect for the needy. They would have circular glass balls, which hung for all to insert a few coins. They were so impressive to me with their music and instruments.

Festive Christmas lights on Water Street in downtown St. John's in the 1950s.

I remember the shoe store, Parker and Monroe, would always have a window display of a Christmas Toyland scene with snow-capped mountains, moving trains, dolls, elves, and everything shiny that would stimulate our young minds. You only saw toys and those displays at Christmas. That window was a definite must-see on our list as we happily discussed our upcoming trip on the United bus, driving along Topsail Road on the way into town.

Once we disembarked from the old faithful United bus, or sometimes Furey's bus, and walked from George Street to Water Street, the elder children received orders from Mom about not straying away and keeping an eye on each other. We couldn't wait to set off to take it all in. Each armed with a few coins in our pockets, we were off on our adventure.

Every year, Mount Cashel Orphanage for boys would hold a raffle on Water Street. You could hear the loud handbell one of the boys would be ambitiously ringing trying to drum up business when you were much further away. There would always be live turkeys in the window, in their stalls with the sawdust on the floor, as one and all waited for them to be won by some lucky raffle winner. They would have spins on the wheels, just like Regatta Day down on the Lake, but the prizes would be Christmas cakes, chocolates, everything for the Yuletide Season, and of course, someone had to win those turkeys. To a young boy's eyes, it was so very exciting.

Next, we visited Woolworth's, with its wonderful bakery on display, Ayre's, the Arcade, and Bon Marche, where Mom would buy the special Christmas patterned oil cloths for the kitchen table. It was December, so we had to have holly berries and wreaths or Santa and his reindeer on our oil cloths. The anticipation of it all was such a joyful emotion, and we all felt so very festive as we helped Mom select those oil cloths while we absorbed every Christmas decoration and colour that was displayed.

Every other year, Mom would also buy enough of another patterned oil cloth to recover the chrome kitchen chairs, which was Dad's job. Those old kitchen chrome sets with the round studded nails were a real sensation at the time. It always amazed me how that particular oilcloth always matched the new paint on the walls. I remember thinking that our mother had a definite eye for home decor!

I'm assuming that all the domestic fuss arose because there would be a week or so of company coming and going and all kinds of get-togethers to celebrate the birth of Christ. Residents wanted their house looking as presentable as their paycheque would allow. Looking back, December seems an odd time to be making household improvements. Given our climate, the house was closed up tight as a drum because of the cold, winter air, but it was Christmas regardless of the temperature.

As the labour for the painting commenced, the furniture would be pulled out, the rugs rolled up, and the doilies on the armrests got washed with a dose of starch. All small children were banished if they couldn't use a brush.

When the home improvement work was finally all complete and in place, I would stand back and look at our new and improved rooms and think to myself, *How fancy are we, and how good do I have it?* By thinking that thought, I actually nailed the situation right on the head. I certainly *was* fortunate and well blessed to share it with my family.

Once that tangley task was complete, with walls somewhat dry and the rooms put back in order, you knew that Mom (and most women), dug out the cast-iron bake pots, and the Christmas fruit-cakes would soon be mixed and put in to bake in the old woodstove.

Those delicious cakes were baked once a year because most households couldn't afford all the fruit, peel, cherries, and raisins that you would need to produce them. And there was never one cake baked, but at least half a dozen at one time.

Poor Mom, I remember, had quite the job to keep some aside for the actual holidays because as children, we were always after her to cut one then and there. The aroma going through the house while they were baking was irresistible. And once it was cut, we always watched with precision for a moment when we could sneak in the pantry. Checking to make sure we weren't seen, we carefully and noiselessly peeled back the layers of wax paper and tinfoil to cut off another little thin, undetectable slice. We did that for a few days until it was all gone! I think Mom knew it was useless to ask who had been in the pantry at her cake, and maybe she did that deliberately because the other cakes were hidden. There were so many of us whittling away at that cake, she would never have known the answer. But we knew that there was more coming later in the month, so we waited patiently.

Along with paint and baked fruit cakes, something else you only saw in December was Purity Syrup. It's still being made today, and I bought it for years after moving out of the family home, simply because it meant Christmas to me. Most people bought the raspberry or strawberry flavour, but it came in a variety of flavours—even lemon.

If you visited anyone's house during the Holidays, you would be given a piece of fruit cake and a glass of syrup. That was the company menu for all youngsters up to about the age of seventeen who dropped by on the pretence of "seeing their tree." It wasn't because you couldn't have more—you just didn't ask for more or even think of it. I think there was an unwritten law somewhere on the island that you made one Christmas visit per house, and you received one drink of syrup and one piece of cake. We were industrious kids, though, because we made sure we visited every house that we could possibly gain entry to.

For the adults, there was always the offer of "shine" in most homes. Now the moonshine that was made discreetly on Paradise Road wasn't 40% alcohol, but more like 100% or more. You could strip the paint off your car with some of that stuff, I'm sure. The word 'potent' hardly describes it accurately.

As I mentioned earlier on, some of us children once tried to make dogberry wine with disastrous results. However, I sampled the actual moonshine at Christmas once or twice, and one gulp was sufficient once you got it gone. But the old timers had no problem with it and tipped it back readily. With one swipe of their sleeve over their mouths, followed by a gasp, you'd receive a hearty wish for your good health at Christmas. They would often go for the second glass and, of course, were never denied as your host dipped the cup into the wooden barrel with the half flap open on the top cover. But in our house, my father never made, drank, or offered moonshine but anyone who visited never left hungry.

There was a continuous flow of company, forever walking in and out the lane of the Pennell house anyway regardless of the month. Oftentimes on Saturdays, post 1960, after we were the proud owners of a coin-operated television set, our living room was filled to the brim with males watching wrestling and trying to duplicate the moves of Whipper Billy Watson and Hardboiled Haggerty. That was always a boisterous few hours, even during the Christmas Season.

With the bright and clean paint job, the new canvas, maybe newly covered chairs, and the odd wreath hung here and there, not to mention the fruitcake and cookies baking, everything contributed to the festive atmosphere. We were surrounded by that wonderfully special feeling with significant religious overtones that only Christmas could bring.

Dad had been given approximately ten acres of land in Paradise by his biological father, Herbert Pennell Sr. That land was well wooded and grew some of the most idyllic Christmas trees you could imagine. Dad, always the entrepreneur, took us along with him on these first weeks in December to help. In the 1950s and 1960s, all the trees were cut locally, and none were imported as they are now.

Those mornings meant an early rise, a hearty breakfast, a packed lunch, and several bottles of hot tea wrapped in a thick wool sock for us for later, compliments of our mother. Off we would go, armed with our saws and ropes in Dad's truck, to that parcel of land. It was a given through the year that come Christmas time, we would visit some part of that ten acres and chop down as many trees as Dad figured we could sell to make some extra money for the upcoming Yuletide Season.

When we were younger and had picked out a certain tree to cut, we would wait for the affirmative nod from Dad indicating that it was a good prospect. Then, out came the saw. The old truck would be full of branches sticking out from every angle, and once we couldn't get another one aboard, and mitts and caps were practically stuck together with turpentine, we headed to St. John's. There was no getting in the open back of the truck now, which was blocked with our trees, so the cab ride was less than spacious once our father and three or four of your growing brothers got in.

We would go to the streets with row housing downtown, so we could avail of as many potential customers as possible. Dad would pull in the old truck, and we would jump out and offload trees so they could stand by the truck and be adequately viewed. Each of us would then spread out and go up to the nearby doors and knock. We waited eagerly for the residents to emerge and scrutinize our selection as we turned the various trees to exhibit them from all angles.

A big, bushy, six-foot tree would sell for $1.50. Can you imagine that now? The smaller ones went for a dollar, and sometimes, the older people asked for a three-footer. We had learned from Dad's experience over the years to always have some smaller ones available. We would nail together two pieces of wood in an X pattern as a stand for those little ones and accept fifty cents total for our efforts. Some people gave you a small tip, and some others would try to barter with you. In that respect, human nature is still the same.

By the time my brothers, Dad, and I had walked in the woods and cut them down, loaded them up, headed to town to put them on display, and then sold a dozen or more, we were well ready for a bite. Sitting on the tailgate in the freezing cold somewhere in the middle of St. John's, or squatting together in the cab of the truck, we would happily take out that hot, sugary tea out of the box and dig into those sandwiches wrapped up in the wax paper. Often Dad had picked up a bag of cheese-cuttings. Nothing tasted sweeter than a homemade sandwich, a cup of tea and half a dozen of Charlie's cheese-cuttings after hours of being a Christmas tree salesman.

It was all such labour-intensive work, but every Christmas, we looked forward to that picnic lunch at the end of the day in the cab of the truck. In retrospect, it warms my heart knowing that both Mom and Dad had the foresight to make it comforting, delicious, and certainly ample for us as growing boys.

As youngsters, our reward actually was that long-awaited feed, and we would be awarded with a quarter,or even fifty cents on a really prosperous day. The remainder of the profits was brought home and put toward provisions for our own Christmas. There were presents to be bought for sure, but food was always given top priority, no matter what month it was.

I often wonder and wish that we had taken account of how many trees we cut and sold in and around St. John's. And wouldn't it be exceptional to get the price, or even half of it, that tree salesmen get today? It was a humbler time for sure.

I'm happy to say that I carried that tradition on with my own offspring. Equipped with a hearty lunch and all the assorted tools, Ches Jr., Bert, Bob, and I (and sometimes my youngest boy, Jerry, and my little girl, Ellen, who could always hold her own with the boys) would board the truck and head into the woods. Once there, they would cut their share of trees for much-needed Christmas money.

I have a very endearing memory of having Ellen work alongside me one time. I told her, after she had put in a productive day, that she was every bit as good a worker as the boys. She told me years later that hearing that from me that day was equivalent to winning an Olympic medal.

My children still talk about those excursions now, when the Yuletide Season is approaching. The best memory was that they didn't have to ask for Christmas money for presents because they had rightfully earned their own and did it together. It was indeed a joint venture, and one where they all prospered.

In my early youth, the Christmas tree would never be decorated ahead of time. We were all taught that once we went to bed on December 24, Santa would arrive, leave some presents for all of us, and decorate our tree in one-fell swoop. He was one busy man! When we hopped up on Christmas Day, it was all complete and looking grand, with presents underneath it for everyone.

However, there were never countless gifts for one child. There would be one gift for each, and most importantly of all, the stockings we had so anxiously hung the night before were still there, but now they were filled with surprises. We weren't used to fruit such as grapes and clementines, or those large nuts that we all loved to get Christmas Day. Most people refer to them as Christmas nuts, even though they're available all year round now. But running out to see the tree all decked out and looking so festive, and grabbing up those stockings and rushing back to the warmth of our beds, was a thrill for me and I would assume all my siblings.

I can see myself and my brothers Herb, Lock, and Wally now, propped up on our bed, quickly spreading out the contents of those bulging stockings, which were, of course, the largest of Dad's wool socks we could find. As soon as we saw what each of us had gotten, the swapping would begin, and the bartering would be well underway. There would always be a little bit of chocolate in there, and it never tasted sweeter. We'd make a mad dash to the back porch for one of Dad's hammers to crack the nuts, and so it began. How Mom ever got our beds rid of all the shells, I don't know.

Every one of us would receive a gift from Santa, and it was usually something practical and necessary, such as pants or shirts, but the toddlers in the family could always expect a doll or a tea set for the girls, or a gun and holster or a game for the boys. The absolute racket in that house at perhaps 5:00 a.m. on Christmas morning would raise the dead, but everyone was helping make that racket, and we were allowed to.

Mom would be holding a baby with one hand and helping someone open their tea set with the other. Dad would sit on the chesterfield while some of us would jump up there next to him and proudly display our new guns or our new jacket, or the girls proudly showed off their brand-new dolls.

Sometime through Christmas Day, after the presents were revealed and the dinner was served and cleared away, Dad would break out his accordion and his mouth organ, and he was equally as skilled on one as the other. My brother, Jim, has both those instruments to this day, and since he was the most musically inclined, I'm glad he does.

There would be a mixture of Christmas carols and Newfoundland jigs and reels ringing out through our house. Countless neighbours dropped by, and sometimes an impromptu dance would start up, thereby giving our brand-new canvas a test. Between that canvas, the newly painted walls, the covered chairs, the festive patterned oilcloths on the kitchen table, the tinsel on the Christmas tree, and an abundance of food and music, it was a happy house indeed. As a child, the whole experience of Christmas, and the anticipation of it, was all just simply marvellous, and as an adult looking back, it still is!

Well, in our little house, as in most houses, the babies came, grew up, and moved on. Some are still in Paradise with families of their own, and others have had to go away. It's my wish that each and every one of those Pennells thinks back and is grateful for all that was home. We didn't always have the latest toys or the newest cars, but we had love in abundance, and that's what is worth remembering.

As the old jokes goes, "I always knew I would get old; I just didn't expect it to happen so fast." And in reflection, I've done lots in my life and seen just as much. I felt every emotion imaginable as I grew up back in that old homestead, and for the most part, those emotions were positive. I consider the life I had in Paradise a fantastic gift from the Lord above, because I was given all the tools to live a good life and the backbone to go out and make it happen.

My parents endeavoured to teach us a healthy work ethic and a strong belief that you were responsible for finding a way to provide whatever was needed to sustain a healthy lifestyle for yourself, and certainly your children. I feel that Walter and Florie both delivered that message in spades. This book is my tribute to both of them.

They tried to instill everything that was good in their children. They also took an active part in their community and were proud to call Paradise their home. I was taught hard work and values, and in child-rearing, that is uppermost, as you pay it forward. I observe my own children, and I feel that I've managed to pass those lessons on.

My parents, Walter and Florie Pennell, in the mid 1980s.

I'll end with a very touching poem that my wife, Jan, wrote for me on my seventieth birthday. I feel that it's a tribute that any man or woman would be proud of, to know that their life could possibly be so tidily summed up.

My fervent wish is that all of you young families who live, grow, and taste the fruits of life in the bigger and modern Paradise today know that your community was built by strong and resilient people. I hope that you will be as content with your life's experiences there as I was with mine.

Having It All

The world became a better place the day that you were born
As Florie wrapped you in her arms that far-off August morn
"He's just like Walter," remarked one and all
"And we hope he's just as kind"!"
How right they were, for as years passed,
Two more alike, you'd never find.

You raised your family, toiled from dawn to dusk,
And gave all that a man could give.
Your children know it was all for them — a prosperous life to live.
You've accomplished it all — are a wonderful husband, a dedicated dad,
And were a generous and caring Son.
You're as gentle a man as ever walked the earth
And if Life is a race, Ches — you've won

CPSIA information can be obtained
at www.ICGtesting.com
Printed in the USA
LVHW040931211221
706818LV00009B/806

9 781039 115309